The Shoestring Library

The Shoestring Library

Sheryl Kindle Fullner

LINWORTH

AN IMPRINT OF ABC-CLIO, LLC
Santa Barbara, California • Denver, Colorado • Oxford, England

Library of Congress Cataloging-in-Publication Data

Fullner, Sheryl Kindle.
  The shoestring library / Sheryl Kindle Fullner.
    p.   cm.
  Includes index.
    ISBN 978-1-58683-520-0 (acid-free paper) — ISBN 978-1-58683-521-7 (ebook)   1. Library finance—United States—Handbooks, manuals, etc.   2. School library finance—United States—Handbooks, manuals, etc.   3. Library fund raising—United States—Handbooks, manuals, etc.   4. Library buildings—Energy conservation—United States—Handbooks, manuals, etc.   5. Library buildings—Environmental aspects—United States—Handbooks, manuals, etc.   I. Title.
    Z683.2.U6F85   2010
    025.1'1—dc22   2010000718

ISBN: 978-1-58683-520-0
EISBN: 978-1-58683-521-7

14 13 12 11 10   1 2 3 4 5

This book is also available on the World Wide Web as an eBook.
Visit www.abc-clio.com for details.

Linworth
An Imprint of ABC-CLIO, LLC

ABC-CLIO, LLC
130 Cremona Drive, P.O. Box 1911
Santa Barbara, California 93116-1911

This book is printed on acid-free paper ∞
Manufactured in the United States of America

For Riley, Iona Lorrene, and Mike Kindle who believed
For Jayma Nichol and Cynthia Klein who encouraged
And for Merle and Paul-Michael Riley Fullner who made it happen

Contents

SECTION 2   THE PHYSICAL PLANT

Figures

About the Author

SHERYL KINDLE FULLNER sold her first articles as a sophomore at Sonoma State University where she worked as a library clerk. After obtaining her teaching credentials, she moved to Corban University in Oregon to be assistant librarian and pursue a master's degree at Oregon State University, Monmouth, and doctoral studies at OSU, Corvallis. A blind date in Washington radically changed her life. She traded academia for a John Deere tractor and a green camouflage kayak. For the past 12 years she has been a teacher/librarian at Nooksack Valley Middle School and writer for professional magazines. She lives in the lap of a national forest with a dormant volcano steaming in the distance and filial bagpipes sounding through the mists.

Introduction

Budgets have plummeted: librarians need an organized resource to fine tune frugality. This book pinpoints specific areas to save money and time while designing a topnotch library. *The Shoestring Library* showcases creative library practices that produce satisfied patrons, rich environments, and confident librarians with minimal funds. More than 400 tips combine with roughly 60 black and white photos for public and private school librarians from pre-schools through college and, by extension, for community libraries.

Caveat

The ideas listed in this book span more than a dozen inventive years at a variety of libraries. An overwhelmed librarian only has the time to do a fraction of these in one year, so start with the most obvious ones. For example, if there is a saddle in the barn, use the "big impact display" hint first with a shelf full of horse books, magazines, and CDs. If there is a tropical fish shower curtain in the linen closet, use it to try out the "inviting temporary spaces" tip. The hints and photos are a jumping off place for each librarian's creativity. Scribble ideas in the book margins while they are fresh and harvest them at leisure. Highlight or sticky note the pages for quick reference.

Getting Started

A lithe Third World librarian sleeps in the upper file cabinet. Whenever there is whining in the library about budget cuts and fewer hours, she climbs down and caresses the aged photocopier, runs a finger along the real chairs, opens books with bright pictures, and says "Ahh!"

 A sense of humor or a sense of perspective is essential to a Shoestring Librarian. Much of the world has poorer libraries than those managed by any librarian in the United States or Canada. An upbeat, uncomplaining can-do librarian will contribute immensely to organizational pride and morale in addition to providing expert information access and training.

Before exploring hundreds of tips for operating freestyle, consider the math of a Shoestring Library. Addition is first. Most librarians would like to add books, databases, seating areas, magazine subscriptions, and other sensible items. When adding anything except books, *reversibility* should be a key consideration. How easy will it be to subtract or reverse changes? When a library moves from desperate to adequate and then graduates to outstanding, edit along the way. Update, recycle, pass on, or discard items that were godsends at the beginning but that no longer fit.

For any change, reversibility should be a key consideration.

Then, multiply effectiveness by trying to have an excellent collaborative relationship with administration and associates. Cartoon librarians run roughshod over coworkers, collect

Figure I.1 Work green, save green

overdue fees, barricade books, and hush learners. The real-life professional librarian leads, defers, cooperates, partners, and above all communicates with administration and colleagues where feasible.

Finally, divide the most arduous tasks among many hands and minds. Solicit opinions, reviews, ideas, help, and suggestions, keeping a positive attitude toward all brainstormers. Wherever and whenever possible, accept advice and give credit, both of which are endearing and durable traits.

Of the 400-plus hints in this book, 114 are included because they conserve resources as well as conserving library funds. Rethink, reuse, repurpose, and recycle are the foundation on which the Shoestring Library is built. Begin with used items and then recycle them again at the end of their use in your library.

The Contingency Fund

Moving from mathematics to economics, the hardest thing for a Shoestring Librarian to create is a contingency or opportunity fund. In some ways, it is easier to get a $1,000 grant than to come up with $50 to spend at garage sales. Most librarians in impoverished areas end up spending their own money to equip their libraries. This first suggestion is simply a way to curtail the damage.

Consider setting aside one percent of annual salary as a maximum spending cap. For many librarians that will be about $100–$125. Have a ceiling for expenditures, to help eliminate guilt over missed bargains. Avoid buying books that support the curriculum because such subsidies give administrators and boards a false picture of what kind of library their budget is providing.

Use the contingency fund for things that will save you time or benefit clients: quickie bulletin boards, CDs, prizes, incentives, clothing from other cultures, decorations, props, lamps, and the occasional flower to uplift staff and patron spirits.

A Shoestring Librarian has to be meticulously circumspect about finances. Here are some well-intentioned fundraisers in which unnamed librarians participate in order to equip libraries. The personal cost-to-benefit ratio is dubious. Volunteer for a charity dunk tank. Kiss a pig. As a private citizen away from the library, give a garden, home or studio tour that costs $6 to attend and $5 to skip: people pay to avoid attending, much like buying a charity ticket to a no-show ball. From the garden, bag up fall fruit or spring vegetables to sell. Return duplicate or inappropriate donated items to stores for cash. Test drive a car in a promotion for a free gift card. Gather aluminum cans to recycle. Listen to a timeshare presentation to get a free sleeping bag to use as a prize. They all work, but are they worth it compared to the amount of time and energy expended?

All that financial finagling is more trouble than mentally allotting a $100 contingency fund and then trying not to spend it all. Keep all sales receipts even for used items. The librarian has to avoid anything that might compromise an audit or reputation.

Instead of financial finagling, allot a $100 contingency fund and then try not to spend it.

Conclusion: Three little letters separate the successful Shoestring Librarian from other professionals: A-S-K. There is always a question on the lips. Follow a Shoestring Librarian past the booths at a regional fair and listen to the questions, nearly one for every vendor. "Could you spare 100 stickers for our library? Could you donate 50 CD holders for prizes? Could you let us have 25 rulers? 20 pencils? 15 pens in our school color? 10 pads of sticky notes?" (Of course, it is a rare person who could audaciously ask for 50 of anything, but if you mention your classes and hold open your goody bag, usually the vendor will drop in several handfuls or even give you a box of items. Often service agencies such as border patrol or police will ask how many you can use, to which it is easier to reply sheepishly, "100?")

"Could you give a free demonstration of your art? Could you bring that miniature donkey to our school for story time? Could you donate one of your books, hats, t-shirts? Wow! Those are fabulous mouse pads!" The winsome supplicant bountifully equips a struggling library.

Three little letters separate the successful Shoestring Librarian from other professionals: A-S-K. There is always a question on the lips.

SECTION 1

Library Management for Tough Times

CHAPTER 1

The Language of Cheap

 Is that your best price? This is a line to use at garage sales or rummage sales. People who are unused to haggling often find it difficult to dicker. It feels confrontational or disrespectful in U.S. or Canadian cultures. A question, on the other hand, gives the seller the chance simply to say "yes" or to lower the price. Another way to ask this is, "Can you do any better on the price?" This is not an ultimatum. If the buyer will not lower the price, you may still wish to buy the item.

 I need to ask your manager a question. In a large chain store, do not waste time talking to clerks. If you have a proposal, go directly to the manager or assistant manager. It is more kind to the clerk to mention a question instead of saying, "I want to talk to the manager," which sounds as though someone is going to get in trouble.

Perhaps you have noticed a damaged item to repair for use at your library or a semi-dismantled fixture that would be perfect for paperbacks. You might make an offer on the entire contents of a closeout or a clearance bin. Be alert to the dates on tags. Script: "I notice this has been on the floor for more than 10 months. I can make you a good offer and free up the space."

 Could you give us a bid on that? Use this with catalog orders. Bids seem like a device used by big-time spenders. How can a tiny order from a Shoestring Library garner a bid? Businesses want you as a customer. If they turn you into an enduring, loyal customer, someday you may make larger purchases. Bids usually have an expiration date. If you have an administration that puts off purchases, this can work in your favor by giving an outside deadline. When you submit your requisition or purchase order to your administrator, put down the list price, the price you have secured by bid, and the expiration date of that bid. This gives your boss a clear picture of how you routinely save money for the district.

 Could you make that retroactive? Whenever you negotiate a good price on a software contract or magazine subscriptions, immediately ask if it could go back several months. Script: "Could you make that retroactive to March?" Every month at the lowered rate is a bonus.

 Can you match this price? Some companies have great prices but poor customer service. Deliveries are delayed. Phone representatives are unhelpful, evasive, or even argumentative. Cataloging is erratic. Ask a supplier that you respect if they can match the unpleasant company's price. Usually your favorite supplier will then ask you to fax a copy of the competing item and price. For the strongest fax image, simply tear the page out of the catalog or photocopy it. If they match the price, write down the confirmation number and the name of the representative. Include these with your purchase order. Again, let your principal know what you are doing.

 Could you throw in _____? When you are making a relatively large purchase, such as a shelving unit, ask for a pair of book supports or some shelf tags under $10 (something inconsequential to a large company but very valuable to you) that relates to the ordered item. Be amiably prepared to be turned down. This is a place for mild humor, "Oh well, I gave it my best shot!" The upside is that you may actually get what you asked for or something similar.

 Beg without groveling. Your own reputation and that of your district is reflected in how you request aid. No one respects someone who whines, bleats, or moans. State your need accurately, briefly, and realistically. Large companies are feeling the pinch as well.

Would you consider a swap? This requires careful orchestration with your administration. It works well within a district where one librarian has a surplus of something another librarian lacks. Legally most schools cannot dispose of or exchange items without considerable paperwork. Do not overstep your minimal authority and be sure to adhere carefully to the chain of command.

The power of praise. When you have to return an item, instead of ranting or complaining, say "This item was not up to your usual high standards and I know you will want to make it right." Postal mail comments generally get better results than e-mails. Unless you are a hardcore penny pincher, skip the next hint.

Use the persistent moron mode. When store advertising is misleading, do not make a scene; make your point. In a very soft voice, say the same thing repeatedly. "Yes, but the coupon says 40 percent off." "Yes, but the coupon says 40 percent off." Do not argue. Most managers cave after the third repetition. Only use this in situations where the ad is obviously not a misprint that would bankrupt the store.

 Let them save face. Recalling that you have to relate to this company for many years ahead, never be obnoxious, but do not hesitate to be relentless. Also, offer alternatives: if the store cannot honor the ad, could the library pick out another item instead at a reduced price? This advice serves for any type of negotiation. Always offer a way for the other party to save face, but also consider that you traveled to their town on your own time with your own gas money because of their ad.

This is what it would take to make me a satisfied customer. Borrow a line from Nordstrom's Department Store. They ask, "What would it take to make you a happy customer?" You can rephrase it, "This is what it would take to make me a satisfied customer." Be willing to bend and be gracious no matter what the outcome. No stomping, eye rolling, or voice raising. Sighs are allowed.

Make your plight known: Can you help me? Create a two-sentence plea: craft it to be swift, accurate, and moving. Deliver it via phone calls early in the morning. Do not leave messages. Here are three samples:

"We are a new school in an ancient building with 257 feet of empty library shelves. Is there *anything* you could do to help us?"

"We are the poorest district in our state, but we are scrambling for every possible free book."

"We have 75 cents per student to spend on library books this year."

Whom do you call and what do you get with this type of plea? This is obviously a desperate measure, not suitable for the average Shoestring Library. Set aside a block of 15 minutes per day, Tuesday through Thursday early mornings for a month to make these calls, roughly three hours of time total. Mondays and Fridays are not good for solicitation. Your computer can generate a list of phone numbers of major library jobbers. (Avoid any company that wants to send you a box of books on approval for inspection. These are frequently older books re-issued with new covers, but not updated.)

Major book suppliers that work with school libraries often have a generous return policy, which means they take a loss on books that librarians find unsuitable for a variety of reasons (usually content or condition). These returned books often have barcodes with other school names attached. They are stamped with that school's property stamp multiple times. The books are bound upside down with the cover facing down and the text facing up. Pages are torn or wrinkled. The book jacket may be backwards. Covers may have defects.

For the distressed librarian who is filling shelves with old issues of *National Geographic,* these peculiarities do not matter. As the library strengthens, replace these books. In the meantime, students get new books and companies get a charity write-off.

CHAPTER 2

Time Management

 Good enough. A popular magazine features two columns side by side: good and good enough. Each month the writer describes the traditional *good* way to do a common job and an alternative shortcut way, which is *good enough*. For those of us brought up on the sentiment, "the good is the enemy of the best," *good enough* sounds like a fast slide into sloth and slackerdom. Actually, *good enough* is a synonym for emancipation.

 Evaluate tasks. Though it sounds like heresy, not all library jobs require perfection. Each individual librarian needs to assess and sort jobs, allocating the most time to those that affect the most people and the smooth functioning of the library. Perhaps the library has a tradition of writing or stamping accessioning information such as date and jobber/publisher inside the frontispiece. Evaluate whether that information is ever used. Does it justify the amount of time it takes? Every librarian has a different tolerance level for simplifying administration.

"Am I doing this for a reason or because it is a tradition? Is it producing an effective result?" These are refrains that need to percolate through a task-filled day.

 Change to patron self-checkout and return. This process can be modified to allow any degree of surveillance desired. For example, a young child may scan a library card or barcode while the librarian looks at the screen and the patron to make sure there is a match. Then the child scans each item. Demonstrate this procedure during library orientation, and lines of 30 students will move through more swiftly than when students hand books to the librarian and receive them back again. It has the advantage of limiting repetitive stress injury as well. Plus, students increasingly live in a self-checkout retail world. They need to know how to manipulate scanners and barcodes.

 Use a Y cable to install an inexpensive USB number keypad on the client side of the circulation counter. Your own scanner plugs into the other side of the Y so that both keypad and scanner are operational at the same time. Some districts use bar-coded student ID cards at every level, but a Shoestring Library may not be able to afford that. Instead, have students, even first graders, type in their student number.

Install a hub. If you are always unplugging one USB to plug in another, ask for a USB hub, which will have five or more USB ports.

Barcode yourself. Because the library computer can generate barcodes, make barcodes to represent all the long account numbers you need to use frequently, such as your local community library card number and the account numbers for your main jobbers. Glue these barcoded numbers to a brightly colored (easily spotted) piece of paper, which you then laminate. Whenever you need to enter those numbers in an online form, scan the paper. Do not be tempted to include any barcodes connected to credit card accounts or social security numbers.

An alternative way to do this is to put these labeled numbers on your computer desktop so that you can select, copy, and paste them quickly.

 Schedule one block of time for your own imperatives. Remember the antique embroidered dishtowels that listed one job for each day of the week, such as Monday/Washing, Tuesday/Ironing? The luxury of scheduling one's own week is long past. Most libraries demand considerable flexibility as jobs, appointments, and meetings filter in from teachers, administrators, and community groups. Still, to maintain a sense of order, pick *one* weekly job that is essential to your peace of mind and write it into your calendar. For example, your indispensable weekly job might be "Clear the Desk" on Fridays. (It can be any day of the week, perhaps your lightest or heaviest day.)

Then do not allow the tyranny of the immediate to interfere with that very personal appointment. Every other day can be flexible and responsive to the building's needs, but Friday would have a planned scrap of inviolate time. Face Monday with equanimity, when Friday has been hectic but prioritized.

Delete forwarded e-mails without reading. Obviously, a few forwarded e-mails are legitimate and have relevant senders/subject lines. However, "Dueling Kitties," "You've Got to See This," "Fantastic Feather Paintings," or "Perfume Scam with Dangerous Ether" go directly into the recycle bin. In the interests of saving other people's time and your reputation, do not forward non–business-related e-mails. The computer, the network, the electricity, and the time to read forwarded materials have all been paid for by employers and taxpayers: reading or sending non–library-related e-mails is a form of waste or theft, but the librarian is the one robbed of valuable minutes. Professionals never, ever send an e-mail that says "please do not break the chain" or "send this to nine of your friends."

Do not be terrorized by phone solicitors. You will easily recognize their opening gambit, "Hi, this is James from Gullible Paperbacks. What's the weather like out there in Washington?"

"James, I never buy books over the phone. Please put me on your 'don't call' list. I am making a note of the date and your company name. Thank you. Good-bye." Spoken all in one breath, no commas, it takes 30 seconds max to deal politely with a salesperson who can then move on to talk to a more likely prospect.

 Avoid a long phone menu. When calling a company, sometimes you can avoid a long phone menu by simply pressing zero twice. The time to experiment with this is *not* after you have already been on hold for half an hour. Some companies use the double zero to bypass the automation and connect directly to a live person.

 Master your library phone's functions. Impoverished schools may have a limited number of phone lines, which means a busy signal is common when you want to make a call. Ask if your school has number to dial that will alert you by ringing briefly when the line is free: in some schools, it is *87. Also learn how to hold and transfer calls.

Do not eat lunch at the circulation desk. As administrators trim budgets, librarians often lose hours. It is tempting to use that precious lunch half-hour to catch up. Lunch in the staff room is a strategic tool too valuable to give up. Nowhere is the adult pulse of an institution more audible than in the staff lounge. You do not have to get on board the complain train, but it is worthwhile to analyze what is being said. Likewise if the staff is excited about new ideas, that comes out in lunchtime conversations as well. Librarians are often isolated, walled in by patrons and media. Shared meals break that isolation and give a broader picture. This is especially important for library clerks and media specialists who may not be included in faculty planning meetings.

Lunch in the staff room is a strategic tool too valuable to give up. Shared meals break isolation, give a broader picture of the institution, and build relationships.

 Go walkabout once a month. That is a great Australian phrase for an information-gathering trip. Carry a spare, even expired, calendar with you and write down hallway displays of student work. This works well for schools and colleges, which tend to have cyclical curriculum content. Walking past 30 rooms in April might garner haiku, tsunamis, Armenia, proletariat, salmon spawning, black holes, burkas, triptychs, and estimating. Back at the library, a quick search of the card catalog shows which subjects need beefing up and also helps to prepare for future Aprils. Depending on the size of the campus, walkabout can take less than 15 minutes and provide an improvised curriculum map.

 Grossology 101! Because seeking free materials is likely to result in hundreds of free items, it is necessary to provide shelf space. If the shelves are crammed full of ancient, unlovely, and uncirculated books, students are an amazing resource as amateur weeders. Confer with a teacher who is sending older students for a booktalk and ask to substitute a community service activity just this once. Alternatively, commandeer a group of willing students (lunchtime students, kids who cannot do gym, children who have not been able to go on a class trip, or a class for which the sub has not yet arrived). Give each student one bank of *fiction* shelves. Have them select the five ugliest, grossest books they can find.

They bring the books up to the circulation desk and hold up one book at a time for your speed inspection. Then they scan the book, you choose delete, and they use a permanent marker to put a slash through the barcode and place the item on the discard book truck. Any books that you want to remain in the collection are reshelved by that student. Fifteen 12-year-old students can weed 150 books in half an hour with only 5 or 6 going back on the shelves. During this exercise, have a bin or box at your feet for tattered popular books that simply need to be replaced with a fresh copy.

Never just write *free*. If you put a free sign on a cart, crate, or chair full of books, be prepared for other staff to appropriate the cart, crate, or chair when the books are gone and the free sign remains. Place the discarded books in a high traffic area with a "free books" sign on the booktruck. Make sure the booktruck is prominently labeled with a large library property sticker.

Students are actually better than adult librarians at spotting gross books. They are not hampered by knowing the book was a classic, that it cost $35, or that it topped state lists. They only care if it looks appealing.

Ongoing student help. An unexpected side benefit of student weeding is that students keep doing it without being asked. You are building a relationship with them and they feel invested. For months after this one-time exercise, students will bring an occasional bedraggled book up to the circulation desk with a succinct comment, "No one would like this one either. The pages are brown. Gross!" They are usually right.

Repurpose Common Objects

Analyze what you already have. You may already own some of the items in this list of hints or be able to purchase them used. A popular saying among the Scots is "Use it up, wear it out, make it do or do without." These hints fall into the "make it do" category, but they can be a charming form of recycling.

Repurpose a paper towel holder. Increasingly, vertical paper towel holders are being designed with heavy bases for one-handed operation. Use one for standard size rolls of Mylar book jacket covers.

As long as you are lurking in the thrift store aisle with kitchen wares, look at the jumble of metal items, various racks, holders, and shelf attachments and try to envision how some could simplify your library chores.

Metal cookbook holders are great for displaying showy books.

Use a modern metal plate drainer as the perfect desktop file. Put decorative file folders where the plates would go. This is superior to standard desktop files because it holds up to 20 file folders and keeps them separated and upright even when you remove one.

Use tension curtain rods to suspend items in windows or door sidelights.

Suspend a shoebag. A clear shoe bag with twelve or more clear plastic pockets can be suspended from a tension rod and used to display natural history items such as shells, cones, or seed pods interspersed with handbooks that cover the same subjects. These shoe bags are often available at dollar stores.

Nab a ping pong paddle. A Shoestring Librarian is often the only staff member in a library that serves hundreds of people. Lines of students are patiently clutching their books when the phone rings with a long-distance call related to tech support, a desperately awaited call. Use a ping pong paddle or pickle ball paddle, prepared ahead of time, with a useful, generic message printed on each side. Hold it up so patrons can see the instructions. "Please sit down and read QUIETLY while the librarian takes this important call."

Paddle as stop sign. Then there are the times when a complex search demands the librarian and one student finish what they have started. The other side of the paddle says "Please, use the clipboard to check out or return your book. Or come back in a few minutes and the librarian will help you when she is finished with this student." Put on any instructions that fit your particular problem. The paddle is easy to find and to hold up, no violent gesticulating required. It helps train students not to interrupt. Store it with the prepared clipboards, within easy reach. (See directions for sub clipboards in chapter 6.)

Repurpose a credit card. Nonfunctioning cards that look and feel like real credit cards often arrive in the mail. They are useful for smoothing the bubbles out of plastic book covers. Auto supply stores also have plastic spreaders, which are larger than the credit cards and fit larger hands. A set of three generally costs a dollar.

Orphan socks. Use a rice-filled black sock (that has lost its mate) as a page weight when cataloging to keep a book open. Black does not show dirt or ink. White works just as well, but gets dingy after a few floor drops. Tie a string firmly around the open end. (You can also throw this in the microwave for two minutes and apply it to relieve neck pain.)

Find the school laundry room. Most schools have a laundry room for the convenience of coaches, cooks, and special needs teachers. Get a spray bottle from the custodian to keep on hand to mist textiles when you remove them from storage to place on display. Run the lightly dampened items through the dryer for a few minutes to remove wrinkles. With close supervision, dryers can also remove wrinkles from vinyl such as graphic shower curtains.

Free plastic heads. Convenience stores often have large figural candy containers that can be solicited for light-hearted free décor. For example, a green alien head can designate outer space books while a king head marks the beginning of cartoon books.

 Exercise step benches are frequent thrift store finds. Choose one in your library colors to serve as a portable podium or dais for student poetry readings or any type of public performance. They are lightweight and can be stored on top of a cabinet.

 Golf pencils are affordable. A box lasts for several years even if student marauders decimate their numbers. Have a supervised student or a volunteer use a miter box to cut some scrap wood to build a fist-sized open box. One-by-four-inch scrounged pine or pallet board works well. Glue the corners together. (Do butt joints with brads if you wish to avoid mitering.) Use a piece of thin paneling for the bottom of the box. Drill three holes (use 5/16-inch drill bit) in one top edge. Insert golf pencils, point up. Cut scrap paper to go in the box. Let students decorate the boxes with nonallergenic poster paints or permanent markers. Similar oak boxes from library supply catalogs are very costly. These are free and students feel a strong sense of accomplishment.

Create signs with photo display blocks. Used, brightly colored, clear acrylic blocks with a wire spiral or alligator clip for photos make excellent signage for the circulation desk. With a word processor, using checkered borders or wide-bordered shapes, create the most common information you need to communicate, such as your name. You can have a stable of blocks to use for different purposes or just change

Figure 2.1 Stored step bench and candy container

out the laminated messages. "Ring bell, librarian is in back room." These blocks are often business promotional giveaways.

 Free placeholders for books. Elementary librarians often use placeholders in the stacks, giving each child a colorful, unique picture to put exactly where the child removes a book for inspection. The two common ways to do this are to purchase placeholders from a library supplier or to make and laminate colorful holders. A Shoestring Library may lack either a laminator or pouches/film to refill it. Ask a local paint store if they will donate 35 paint sticks to your library. Paint sticks are durable and hold their shape when stuck between books. To distinguish between children, use bold, colored markers to write a different word on each stick or a design that even pre-literate children can recognize. At the end of the year, you may need to replace a few grimy sticks.

Measure your bulletin board. Cut a string four inches longer than the board. Coil the string in a metal candy tin with a hinged lid. When you send students to get bulletin board paper, outstretched arms never communicate as well as the string or a used metal tape measure. Ask for a 12-foot tape via the newsletter. Label the tape measure with your library name. While tape measures sometimes disappear, old string in a tin is immune to theft.

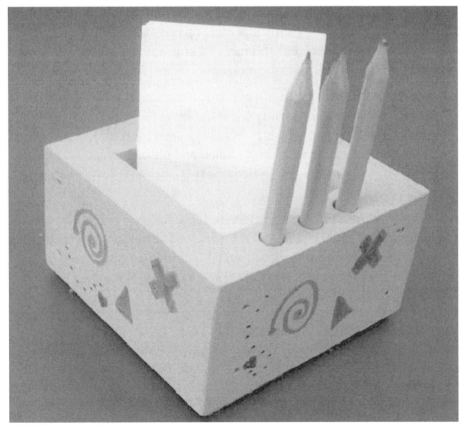

Figure 2.2   Student-built pencil holder

Big-Impact Display Items

 Bulletin boards are time eaters. Evaluate whether bulletin boards are accomplishing what you intend. In general, high bulletin boards (bordering the ceiling) are more decorative than informative. They satisfy the librarian's need to create a dynamic environment with movement through a calendar year. For some, bulletin boards literally hang over their heads: one more chore to complete in an overburdened schedule. For others, bulletin boards are an exhilarating creative outlet: the flash of scissors, the rain of colored paper, and several happy students push-pinning their way to glory.

 Pin up multiple background papers at one time. To speed up bulletin board production, put up several different background papers at one time in a variety of colors; push pin the corners. This eliminates multiple trips to the supply closet of the school and it is quicker to measure and trim three backgrounds at once. As you tire of one color after several months, remove it to display a fresh sheet. Green butcher paper might begin life in February as a 3-D garden of paper daffodils and then morph into a background for March leprechauns and gracefully exit in April as the backdrop for a composting emphasis for Earth Day. Then it is time to tear it down to reveal a new color.

 Match bulletin boards to paper sizes. Do not be tempted to purchase a bulletin board which is a different width than the butcher paper that will be covering it. The extra display space is not worth the piecing and fiddling.

 One quick way to deal with bulletin boards is to take them down. Perilous times demand strenuous measures. Some libraries have four or five bulletin boards, which is a crushing number to keep current. Remove several to storage. Have the resulting holes in the wall spackled and painted. If your administrator wishes to be involved in small decisions like this, explain that just leaving them empty and up is not a good option. Empty boards shout two phrases: "lazybones" and "fill me." Tacking a few photocopied book jackets to an acre of burlap never has quite the motivating power that one hopes.

 Avoid piddly jobs. Often in the first year after certification, teacher-librarians find themselves cutting out hundreds of little bitty leaves, snowmen, or cherries for a bulletin board edge. Then they discover packages of leaves, snowmen, and cherries that they can purchase. The leaves still need to be attached and ultimately unattached and stored. The sooner a librarian masters fast bulletin boards, the more time there is for teaching information access skills.

 Cut out huge letters. These first two suggestions fall into the go big category. Giant, three-foot-tall butcher paper letters, 11 × 17–inch construction paper letters, or 8 × 11–inch Astrobrite letters fill up a board speedily. Enlarged photocopy captions are even speedier. Instructions for both of these methods follow.

The Photocopied Bulletin Board

To convey content, type brief captions in a bold, sans serif font such as **Arial Black** or a bold, novelty font such as Chiller or Curlz MT at size 200 instead of font size 12. Only one or two words will fit on a page. Use the landscape, horizontal page orientation. Then photocopy your page onto 11 × 17–inch paper enlarged to roughly 165 percent. To make quickie posters, use the portrait orientation. (A five-color highlighter pen adds splashes of color for posters.)

Fold and Cut Letters

Most letters in the alphabet are symmetrical in at least one direction. To begin, cut paper of any color into rectangles for the width and length needed. Letters can be tall and thin or short and wide. Follow the diagrams below for each letter. Some, like S, Z, and N, cannot be folded and cut.

NOTE: Most letters take up about the same amount of space, with the exception of "M" and "W". Make the paper for these letters a little larger.

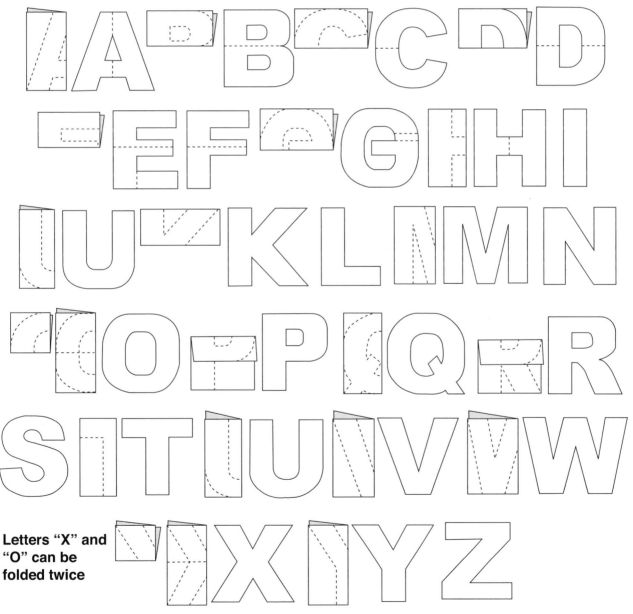

Letters "X" and "O" can be folded twice

Figure 2.3   Fold and cut letters

Giant captions. Another way to handle a bulletin board is to use it as a caption for a big-impact display item. When it is time to feature adventure books, haul in a kayak to place on top of several shelves or tables, shoved together. (Do not place a kayak on the floor where students might try to sit in it to its detriment.) Use the quick fold and cut method to snip out a two-foot-tall caption "White Water Reads." All three E's are cut at one time with a stack of three pieces of paper. Choose media/books that go with each display piece.

 Pond boat. If you use a large pond boat, couple it with the phrase "Sail Away with a Playaway." If you do not have Playaways, substitute sailing adventures or biographies.

 Canoe. A canoe, bolstered by the words "Silent Paddles" in immense letters, conjures up Native Americans. If the canoe is too large for your space, just display paddles.

 Inflatables. A colorful air mattress suspended from the ceiling invites readers to "Float Away With a Summer Novel." Use all kinds of inflatables. Summer water toys often include huge orca whales and dragons. Inflate them using the air compressor in the bus garage.

 Snowboards and skis. Moving away from the nautical, put up skis, snowshoes, or snowboards. Dangle them in front of your bulletin boards. Some ski boots and ski poles on the display shelf along with winter action books or tapes take less than 10 minutes to arrange. Or suspend several pairs of ice skates against a dark blue or pale blue background.

 Write with spray snow. After the holidays, use a marked-down can of spray snow to create a snowdrift and a caption on the background, which is much easier to clean up than spraying it on glass. You can write cursive with snow just as you do with spray paint.

 Ask sports people. Via the school newsletter or in personal conversations with sports enthusiasts, ask people to donate old skis or snowboards. Store them easily in a backroom corner and use year after year with different crops of books—one year with alpine mysteries, another year with Olympic biographies.

 Wheelbarrow. A wheelbarrow lends itself to displaying agriculture or farm-themed media such as *Little House on the Prairie* DVDs, country western CDs, or tractor books. While it is tempting to add a few hay bales for ambience, the clean-up is not worth it.

 Bicycle. An old-fashioned bicycle with a basket can hold nostalgic books, while a mountain bike can promote action books. Borrow a unicycle to fix securely to a wall above students' reach or chain to a table. If you have a student who can both ride a unicycle and wave a book at the same time, you have a stellar booktalk visual.

Saddle. Promote perennial favorite horse books with a full western or English saddle on a sawhorse. Drape a piece of butcher paper over the sawhorse first. Add call numbers.

Wheelchair. A wheelchair provides a flat surface for media with a medical theme. Lay a spare shelf across the arms of the wheelchair on which to stand books. Several more books can go on the seat and on the footrests. Lock the wheels.

 Transport large items. Big-impact display items may save bulletin board time, but they present their own challenge in terms of transport. Whenever possible ask the people who are lending the item to drop it off at the school. The effectiveness of using the big item is in its novelty. Do not do several big items in a row. Merely use one for each season.

 The perils of borrowing. It is actually easier to borrow huge items that are too big for students to harm than to borrow hand-held artifacts that students can drop, break, or remove. Temper the convenience of a large display with caution. Only borrow or use things that are not priceless or limit big items to your own belongings

Gear. Gerard Manley Hopkins celebrated all "trades, their gear and tackle and trim," and so can the librarian. Run a four-foot heavy dowel or closet rod through the sleeves and shoulders of any uniform such as that of a firefighter, forest ranger, or sheriff and suspend it from the ceiling or in front of a blank bulletin board in an appropriate color. Children and teens enjoy sketching and cutting out orange and yellow flames to superimpose on a red background for a firefighter or forestry emphasis. This theme promotes career or fiction books as well as picture books.

College sweatshirts. Particularly for grades 6 through 12, feature college sweat-shirts on dowels. Colleagues are a good source for borrowed alumni clothing. Five or three shirts make a good splash to combine with a college or career emphasis. (Uneven numbers of display items follow the Japanese aesthetic for pleasing arrangement.)

Textiles. Use pushpins to attach textiles to a bulletin board, scrunching fabric to create a more three-dimensional board. For Mother's Day, use two aprons, a police utility belt, a lineman's belt, and a canvas tool belt. Ask students to paper the board with praises for people who have nurtured them. This is a painless way to create an interactive display.

Primary resource artifact. Students are learning earlier to distinguish between primary, secondary, and tertiary resources. When looking for big-impact display items, think history. Great grandpa's Works Progress Administration (WPA) fire suppression kit is not serving a purpose in the attic. Feature it against solid piece of butcher paper with WPA cut out in large letters to connect students not only with history but also with relatives.

 Substitute a shape for a hole. When doing fold and cut letters that have openings such as the "P" and the "A," forgo a hole and substitute a shape such as a pine tree to go with your content. A photocopied caption lets students know what WPA stands for and that in some places, black WPA or CCC workers *built* parks but *could not picnic* in them.

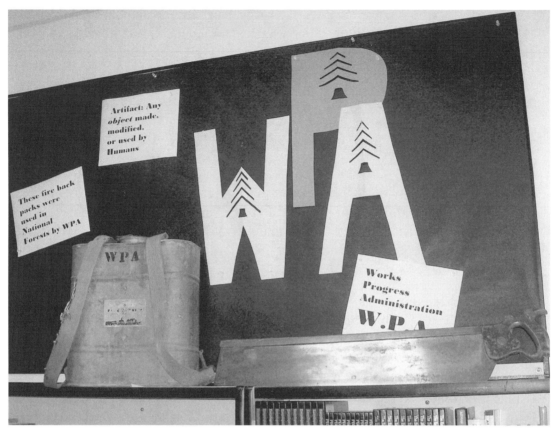

Figure 2.4   WPA artifact with fold and cut letters

Interactive. When exhibiting 20th-century artifacts, make them interactive by posting a question both on the board and in the school newsletter. "Did anyone in your family work for the WPA or CCC during the Great Depression? E-mail us your story!" Post abbreviated answers as free ephemeral wallpaper on library computers.

Create Inviting Temporary Spaces

About twice a year, stir things up by creating a mini-environment in the library. Craft a space where students can feel a sense of enclosure while still being constantly observable for safety reasons.

Suspend a garage sale mosquito net from the ceiling. Drape the hem of the net around several chairs or vinyl bean bags. Readers are completely visible but have a delightful sense of seclusion. Mosquito nets may be plain white, but frequently come in bright colors embellished with flowers or ribbons. This does not diminish their attraction for boys as well as girls. The high school football players choose this space as readily as kindergartners. A beefy fullback grinning at you and saying, "Look, we are princesses!" is ample reward.

Shower curtain. Attach a clearance sale shower curtain to wire strung at an eight-foot height across the library. Children's or teens' shower curtains often have age-appropriate graphics such as unicorns, race cars, or tropical fish, all of which lend themselves to book tie-ins. Choose curtains that are transparent, rather than opaque, to keep all students in view.

 Tent. Put up a one-person toss tent that has large see-through mesh areas for single student use. This is a special privilege tent to use as a reward. It should be near the circulation desk and clearly labeled "One Student: One Book." If your school has a Playaway or a Kindle, reward its use combined with the tent. Avoid the use of fabric pillows or cloth beanbags to reduce lice transfers.

Beaded curtains. Beaded curtains generally are for doorways. Hang two sets at right angles near a corner to create a defined, four-walled space. Bead or shell curtains, and their cousins made of plastic, frequently show up in thrift stores. The beads should not reach the floor. Hang the hem just below students' line of sight. They will still feel mysteriously secluded.

Hula skirts. Hula skirts of the variety used as party favors can create a tropical feeling arranged overhead in an open square. Since the bottoms of the skirts are six feet from the floor, there is no concern about concealed students, but it still gives the feeling of an exotic hut for about five dollars.

Fabric gazebos. Many types of portable cabana or gazebo structures are sold for use in yards and then stored away for the winter. They usually consist of a nylon or canvas roof supported by aluminum telescoping legs. Borrow one of these to unfold in a cleared library space. Avoid the ones with screen curtains attached because, unfortunately, poking holes in a taut screen has as much fascination for students as picking at scabs. Use the space for kicking off a summer reading program.

Rearrange a few stacks. Sometimes librarians long to rearrange the stacks in a more efficient or intuitive pattern only to be stymied by their mass. Stacks made from laminate and medium-density fiber board (popular in the 1970s and 80s) are intimidating, seemingly welded to the library floor and as daunting as the Great Wall of China.

Consult with administrators, maintenance workers, or custodial staff about the possibility of breaking a few units down for repositioning. The standard format for these shelves is several banks of shelves screwed (not glued) together and topped by one long continuous surface that makes them appear to be a single unit. Have the carpenter examine to see if the banks beneath can be separated. (Cut a strip off a transparency and slide it between the vertical cracks to check for gluing.)

Caution. Be warned, however, that even if stacks are easily divisible, the floors underneath may be devoid of the current carpet. Exposed carpet edges or bare subfloors present hazards to wheelchair users, book trucks, and meandering students. A good time to divide old shelving is when replacing old carpet. If you are in the position of contributing to the design of a new or remodeled library, make every effort to defeat economy motions that would take new carpet only up to the edges of existing stacks. Industrial carpet tiles are a great solution to reconfiguring library stacks.

Save Time and Money at the Circulation Desk

 Recorded booktalks. While students are waiting in line to check out, play a *free* online first chapter of a recorded book from a site such as Random House in lieu of a booktalk. Play it loud! You may need to install speakers. Ask your tech person if any are in storage.

 Fragrance samples. Annoying fragrance samples in magazines are very popular with both male and female patrons when trimmed into free bookmarks.

 Date due stamps are expensive to replace. When you reach December of the last year available on your stamp, carefully remove the year band. If you leave it in place, students tend to keep moving it to years past and complaining about the problem. Also check to see if your stamp manufacturer sells replacement bands or refurbishes stamps.

Measure twice, chuck once. On 11 × 17–inch paper, photocopy a yard stick/meter stick. Cut out the paper copy and cover it with broad library clear tape to attach it to the top of your keyboard tray (under your gel wrist rest). It is a handy reference whenever you need to mark media for call number placement. Choose a ruler that includes centimeters because many publishers describe their books metrically. It is disheartening to receive a book purchased with limited funds only to find out that is either too large for the shelves or so small as to be constantly lost.

Know the maximum height of your shelves. At the same time, measure the height of your fiction, nonfiction, and reference shelves and aim labeled arrows at the paper ruler to indicate the maximum those shelves can accommodate.

 Eliminate book guilt. A Shoestring Librarian has limited time to order books, a task squished in between teaching keyboard skills to the first graders and Internet site evaluation skills to the fifth graders. Consequently, award book lists are often the default of choice. A friendly company sends an e-mail touting the most recent state award winners for elementary schools. One precious purchase order later, the books are on their way. Book box opening day at the Shoestring Library is a quasi-religious event with students in a state of ecstasy. While the librarian is looking for the box cutter, last used on last year's single order, the students have ripped open the box with their bare hands. Squeals fill the air. The science books sit in a lonely pile while fiction is passed eagerly from hand to hand.

When things calm down and the students have left, the librarian goes through the box deliberately, handling each book with joy . . . except the four-inch-tall handbook of flags. Picking up one book praised as a page-turner, he scans the first page. Rats! Purple condoms on page one. The state list said this was a terrific book but the local community has expressed neither a preference for colored condoms nor a desire for the third graders to know about them. As for the four-inch-tall flag book, it will disappear behind its brethren, lost. Two books totaling $50 represent one-tenth of the book budget.

The librarian naturally feels crushed: all that shoestring skimping and saving only to waste 10 percent. This is *unearned guilt.* If there were sufficient time to evaluate or even handle books, he would not have made the mistake. The librarian is not responsible for the shrinking library workday.

 To redeem this problem, offer the books to another library. Books should flow freely up and down across grade levels between district libraries. The books might be a good fit for the middle school or the high school, but perhaps neither of those two schools has any "too young" books to swap.

 Reciprocity of similar items. Option one: simply wait and let reciprocity occur naturally, when the high school librarian orders a graphic novel only to find out it is a picture book that high school students would be mortified to carry.

 Trade for something different. Option two: ask for something in place of the book. Perhaps the high school library has an excess of four-inch tape or Mylar book covers. Swap. Districts may have strong rules in place about shifting large resources, but this simple, occasional materials swap is common in most districts.

 Humility. Of course, all this requires an atmosphere of friendly collaboration and humility. If one librarian is always ready to find fault, criticize, or blame, it stifles the possibility of helping each other nonjudgmentally. Likewise, if a librarian is a perfectionist, it will be hard for that person to admit book order mistakes. Work to create good will, but if that is not possible, limit your swapping base to include likeminded people.

Call number placement. If you are beginning a new library, put the call numbers about one quarter inch from the bottom of the spine instead of the common two inches. This ensures uniformity while eliminating tedious measuring. This one decision saves thousands of minutes over time; no ruler, no marking the spine. Also, that quarter inch buffer makes the label last longer because it is not coming into contact with the shelf.

Pirate the Dewey numbers. Most automated programs allow books to be scanned in by ISBN or title in order to acquire thorough catalog entries. Sometimes, the book or other media is not in the provided database. It is reasonably easy to do a quickie cataloging job on fiction: title, author, ISBN, and call number. Nonfiction demands more, specifically an accurate Dewey number. If there is no time or training to do proper cataloging, pirate the Dewey numbers from a public library online catalog. Then enter the title and author in all capital letters, so that when you scroll through your catalog later, it will be easy to pick out the entries that need updating. (Professionally cataloged items always have both upper and lowercase letters.)

 Reduce the number of stored, uncataloged books. It is a matter of pride to have all items thoroughly cataloged, but a Shoestring Librarian needs to ask a harder question: are uncataloged books, squirreled away in back rooms, under counters, in boxes, doing anyone any good? Is it more important to have books cataloged or to have them in student hands?

Are uncataloged books, squirreled away in back rooms, under counters, or in boxes, doing anyone any good?

 Here is the most outrageous hint in this book: Cataloging on demand. When all your scrounging efforts result in hundreds of fairly new paperback fiction, it can be overwhelming. What should you catalog first? You will recognize the cream of the crop and easily deal with those, but what about unfamiliar titles and authors? How can you choose which ones are most likely to be snapped up by eager readers? Do not choose. Let them choose.

 JIT. The production strategy called "just in time" works for car and furniture and grocery companies all over the world. The JIT model does not create the product until there is demonstrated demand. Take the same approach to cataloging free books. Put them in a bin with a catchy name: "Catalog on Demand," or "Bin There, Ain't Done That." On the sign, explain that bin books go to the end of the checkout line because it takes a little more time to enter them into the computer. JIT books use a lean library model in which no excess cataloging occurs: only desired books, demanded books, and books that are already on hand receive a barcode. Incidentally, you can acquaint your students with this common economic model. You are not talking about excess inventory of books, but rather excess cataloging of undesired books.

Once a bin book gets a barcode and is checked out by a student, it morphs into a shelf book upon its return. It already has a barcode identity, title, and author—the bare bones. When it returns, it has the cachet of the chosen. Add a spine label and ISBN. Hit MARC look-up. If it shows up, great! If not, it is "good enough." This was an orphan book, taken in by strangers. It does not aspire to full cataloging.

 Someone else's doorstep. At the end of a month or a week, remove any unchosen books that remain in the bin and park them on someone else's doorstep. Put them out as free books so students can build up their own libraries or teachers may pick them for classroom libraries. Refill the bin with a fresh batch.

Fraternal twins. If you are the fortunate recipient of book fair books, they often are not available in MARC look-ups, especially if they are recent titles. (Cataloging is offered for a price by the book fair company, but a Shoestring Library cannot afford that hefty fee.) If they are part of a series, choose the closest match and type "SIMILAR TO" in capital letters. You are identifying the book as a "fraternal twin" to a known cataloged book, similar to, but unlike. Do type in the accurate title. This will give your patrons access to quick general notes for searching without you having to type in lots of details. At the same time, it flags the entry so you can try for a MARC record later.

Mindless job for a sick day. Most librarians occasionally come to work unwell (but not contagious). Scrolling through 500 entries looking for "all caps" entries and pressing control-M (or whatever keystrokes obtain MARC records in your automated system) is a mindless job that is good for what ails you. Jot down which batch of call numbers you finished so that you can go on to the subsequent numbers on the next "under the weather" day. If you have an online library system, copy and paste an ISBN or title to find updated Marc records that were not available when the book was first added to your library.

Shoe bank. When students ask to borrow scissors or rulers, ask them to leave a shoe in your shoe bank. No one gets on a school bus with one shoe. They will inevitably remember to return your supplies. Students may prefer to leave a watch, ring, or other jewelry, but the risk of theft or other complications is too great.

Shop widely. If your school belongs to a purchasing consortium, do not limit your ordering to the stationery or library sections. For example, the school nurse section will have alcohol towelettes, tweezers, and disposable gloves, all of which have library applications such as cleaning keyboards, removing tiny bits of torn paper from printers, and handling glue projects.

Long throat staplers. Extra-long (18-inch) staplers facilitate quick bulletin boards by allowing you to attach lettering, posters, pictures, book jackets, and photocopied captions to precut butcher paper *before* posting it on a bulletin board. If an object is just barely out of reach of the long stapler, gently fold the background paper without creasing it and feed it into the stapler to gain those extra inches. Pre-attaching materials works well for bulletin boards that are up high. Some cork bulletin boards do not accept pushpins well. This method bypasses that problem. It is also faster than using tape or glue.

Spray mount adhesive. Spray mount adhesive is quicker and faster to apply than rubber cement. Since it adheres better, items do not fall off a bulletin board mid-month. The inherent difficulty here is overspray. If you lay pictures out on unfolded newspapers to spray them, the adhesive drifts onto nearby carpets, tiles or table surfaces. This may not be immediately apparent, but after a few days, the square outline of the newspaper edges will be visible as the glue attracts dirt. To avoid this, place an item face down in a wastebasket with a plastic liner and spray deep inside the wastebasket. It corrals all the overspray.

Huffing is a major concern on most campuses, so do not do this when students are present. Protect yourself from inhaling the fumes for safety's sake.

Titlewise. The single most valuable free catalog/circulation tool is Follett's Titlewise. The regional representative will tell you how to very quickly submit your existing library for analysis electronically. Your library does not have to be online to do this. Titlewise then divides your collection by Dewey number to show you which specific areas are under-represented and which books are aged. With practically no effort or time on your part, you have instant access to statistics that show that you are far off the national mark for biographies, or that the five volcano books that you thought adequate are actually 15 years old and current volcanology has rendered them obsolete.

Of course, Follett, in the business of selling books, is glad to suggest exactly the titles that will bring your collection up to date. They *do* require that you have a current account with them, but that can be satisfied by ordering a few books per year. Evaluate the many services they have to offer and then send your remaining book orders to them or wherever you prefer.

Avoid extra trips to the library. Consider a subscription to gotomypc.com. This service will allow you to access your work computer remotely, even in other states or countries. The company sometimes offers a *one-time, one-month free trial.* Gotomypc.com is available by the month and may be particularly useful during summer break or during an extended illness. Chemo may leave you with no energy for student contact, but you might be anxious to complete grants or book orders at your own pace from home.

If your library is not on the Internet, this can be especially helpful for book orders when you run into an amazing sale while away from your school. It also allows you to access all word processing files, spreadsheets, e-mails, and publishing just as you would if seated at your work desk. As districts pare budgets to the bone, some librarians may choose to negotiate telecommuting options. This service even works with dial-up Internet, slowly. (Telecommuting does not create smog.)

Print the error screen. Whenever you encounter an error in any application, capture the error message as a screen save and paste the screen into a word processing document. Then e-mail the screen capture to your district or building tech person or your automation guru. When technical support people can see exactly what you are encountering, their response is faster and more accurate. (Remember they may also see scraps of other open files if you have not pressed Alt, so be discrete.) Next, print your inquiry and their response and file it in your solutions notebook as well as filing it in your electronic solutions folder. Of course, new methods for screen captures develop constantly and they differ between PCs and Macs. Consult your technology person for a *how to* lesson.

File your solutions. If you have not kept track of solutions in the past, now is a good time to start. An electronic solution folder is easier to search, while a printed solution may be quicker to access.

Identify poor shelvers. Ideally anyone shelving books in your library has been thoroughly trained, but realistically a Shoestring Librarian is drowning in unshelved materials and grateful for people who can lunge in the general direction of a Dewey number. One way to gauge how accurate your volunteer shelvers are is to photocopy the spines of five difficult books and then salt those books among the returns. If volunteers shelve these abysmally, you can diagnose where some gentle, nonconfrontational tutoring is necessary.

ABCD routing carts, crates, or shelves. If your library is fortunate enough to have several spare book trucks, use them to facilitate routing. For example, label one cart "Automation," another "Book Jackets," and a third "Call Numbers." If you do not have book trucks, label shelves, or crates with the same names. Move books through the trucks or shelves by putting a large sticky note on each book. An "A" printed on the sticky note means that the cataloged book is now in your computer's *automation* system. "B" means that the Mylar *book* jacket or vinyl cover is attached or that none is needed. "C" indicates *call* number created and attached. "D" stands for *done* and may include final steps such as a property stamp or genre label.

Work on books in any order. If a volunteer is suddenly available to do fiction call numbers, wheel the "C" cart to the work area, adding books from other carts if needed. A "C" is hand printed on each sticky note as the volunteer types and attaches the call number to the book. At the end of the volunteer's shift, move the books to a different cart for another step in the accessioning process. Keep the automation cart close to your own desk since you will do most or all of the cataloging. When the sticky note has accumulated A, B, C, and D notations (not necessarily in that order), the item is ready to shelve.

Charitable gifts and small grants. Librarians who work partial days probably do not have time to go after labor-intensive grants (though it is exhilarating). Keep your eye on newspaper articles that describe charitable gifts given by nearby organizations. Retired teachers, service clubs, and even garden clubs donate to worthy projects. Whenever you see a description of their generosity, write a short letter to describe your *own* library's needs.

A tiny donation of $100 can be a tremendous morale booster to the librarian who is struggling for essentials. These gifts usually have no strings attached, no lengthy reports to file, and no accounts to manage. They are simply a check in the mail.

CHAPTER 3

Free Education

Pump up your résumé. Free education does not necessarily propel a person toward a degree, but it does pump up a résumé and increase a librarian's knowledge base.

Take a class. Many libraries are limited by law or by unions to a specific pay scale. Negotiation, bonuses, and incentives may not be apparent. Nevertheless, tuition is one unmentioned asset worth pursuing. Ask your supervisor for tuition and materials fees for a class that will specifically benefit your patrons. Community college classes in computer skills equip you to pass on those skills to browser users. If you have even one student who uses sign language, opt for a signing course. With a sizable immigrant or First Nation population, pursue a language or an English language learners program. Build your résumé at the same time you are making yourself more valuable to your employer.

Ask your union. Check with your union representative to see if professional development money is included in the union contract. Find out what the allowed maximum is per year. If your library is part of an organization in dire financial straits, you will be both wise and kind to avoid the maximum. Pick a median figure and take as many courses as possible. Taking even one course per year prepares for possible layoffs or job changes. Routinely broaden and update skills.

Seek out clockhours at events. If an employer offers or agrees to pay for attendance at a library convention, media specialists conference, or children's literature event, find out if clock hours or credits are available and purchase those yourself.

Ask for a fee waiver. If a local college, especially a community college or tech school, is offering a course that would enable you to enrich your patrons, write a letter asking for a fee waiver. Present your case like a lawyer. Be persuasive. Explain your financial circumstances. Describe how the course would benefit your patrons and the very community from which the college recruits its students. A fee waiver fits in with most college mission statements (available online): by helping you, they will be helping many. Quote a line from their specific mission that best matches your request.

For example, if your library has twice the number of Native American students as the state average, a native drumming or First Nations language course might give you unique access to those students. Use statistics effectively. Dropout rates for Native students are currently at over 49 percent in some locales. That demands extraordinary library measures. Obviously, a fee waiver request is a rare, one-time request. It is not a way to acquire a BA.

Document any free online courses you take. Ask for an electronic certificate or statement of completion. At a minimum, record the URL, date, and time. Microsoft has many free online courses. State libraries often have excellent online courses. Ask colleagues for their recommendations.

Take the tutorials attached to your own computer programs. This seems obvious, but often with the scarcity of time, librarians just plunge in and hope to wing it. There are degrees of proficiency, and the tutorials can help you master and explore the capabilities of your programs. Most school districts move equipment around, with the more sophisticated computers starting at the high school or honors level and then filtering down, eventually reaching middle school and elementary libraries. It is common to arrive on the day before school starts to find a utterly unfamiliar piece of used equipment sitting where your formerly trusty computer sat. Even the power on button may prove hard to locate. In the first few weeks of school, try to arrange your calendar to include exploratory time with any new equipment. Though it is a hectic and demanding month, you will ultimately save time by investing time in machine mastery.

eHow and wikiHow. While the tutorials that support your computer are a good choice, sometimes a quick venture onto the Internet will show you how to accomplish a task. Both eHow and wikiHow are sites that give step-by-step instructions for some projects. The quality of writing and information on these sites is erratic, but they can be genuinely useful. For example, "How to Add Borders to a Microsoft Word Table" rates 4½ stars, while the site for " How to Teach the Dewey Decimal System" barely ekes out a single star.

(Sometimes these sites offer compensation for writers: one cent per hit. The amount of time required to create a popular how-to article and limited demand make it unlikely that your library hint will break even, but it is a worthy challenge.)

Keep a log of any free webinars that you attend. A webinar is a seminar offered online. Usually there is a registration process. View webinars directly related to your library expertise during your paid work hours. The difference between a webinar and a regular tutorial is that most webinars offer an interactive opportunity. Real-time questions may be called in and answered during the webinar, like a conference call. Many schools have a very limited number of phone lines. If your webinar requires telephone access, schedule your participation so that it does not compete with the school phone service if possible. You can participate when no major classes are scheduled for the library. It is helpful to have a set of headphones to reduce distractions since students probably will still be using the library. If you have a group of people who need to see a specific webinar, contact the trainer to possibly schedule a mutually agreeable time.

Caveat. Before promoting or hosting a webinar for other staff, view it ahead of time to see if it is well done: some are abysmal.

Ask a school secretary to dial long distance. A Shoestring Library may not have access to all varieties of free 800 phone numbers. For example, some webinars use a free 877 number that may be restricted for most phones outside the school office. (Some vendor numbers also feature 877.) To work around this problem, ask your office secretary to dial the number for you and patch you through.

Fill empty dialog boxes. When you register for any company's webinar or other online services, the form may ask you for membership, account, or subscription numbers, which penuriously you do not have. Instead of leaving those boxes blank, which may abort your sign-in, try typing anything in the dialog box such as "nothing," "none," or "don't know." That is frequently sufficient as long as your e-mail address and name are correct.

Webcasts. If a webinar seems daunting, one alternative is a Gale guided tour or webcast *article* that reads itself to you, pointing out salient features with moving arrows and highlights. These articles are terrific to use with small groups of 20 students. Project your computer image onto a library screen so that students can follow the action. The related Cengage guided tour article gives them step-by-step instruction for effective searches. Access the webcast at any time with no phone connection. Your library probably already has some Gale reference works: the Gale Company has applied the same expertise to training students and librarians to access online reference materials; good quality teaching modules that you do not have to create improve your level of service without encroaching on your time.

Take advantage of tax-supported public library databases. Suppose your library cannot afford any databases. Demonstrate to your students how to use a city or county library database most efficiently. For example, if a county library subscribes to Gale's Health and Wellness database, students can log on using their own public library card number. They can find data that is excellent for reports, but this also allows students to explore health issues privately. Don't forget to log Cengage articles into *your* education file as well.

Evaluate listserv use. In the past, listservs were touted as a professional tool of choice for self-education. With current time constraints, many librarians have removed themselves from all listservs. A listserv is a device or program that e-mails information to a large, specialized group of people at once. A listserv may arrive in your inbox as individual e-mail messages (dozens per day) or as an index of messages from which you choose the most likely ones to request or as a compilation of threads about a specific topic.

Free listserv. Frequently there is a cost attached to a listserv, such as the membership fee for belonging to a state or provincial library association. A Shoestring Librarian very likely has let all such memberships lapse for lack of funding. Still, there is a manageable and helpful free listserv: LM_Archives. This is a collection of past postings arranged by either date or thread topic. You can visit this site to see what other librarians are currently tackling or to see if someone has posted a question for which you also are looking for an answer. Caveat: only click on items that say "HIT" in capital letters. The others are questions without answers, something that a Shoestring Librarian already has in abundance.

Nings are gaining in popularity among some groups. These are networking sites created by individuals to attract a specific set of users. For example, a group of state or provincial teen librarians might decide to have a Ning to exchange information about electronic reads. Two problems can arise with a Ning: first, how do you identify and attract likeminded librarians? Second, how do you set up, police, and maintain the site with a minimum of time and effort? Neither of these problems are insurmountable to enthusiastic techies. Of course, newer ways of connecting are evolving even as this is written.

Delicious.com. A simple alternative to a Ning is the fabulous free resource, Delicious.com (formerly del.icio.us). This tool allows you to store all your favorite bookmarks online, instead of tying them to one particular computer at home or at work. Delicious can save all your hardworking, daily use bookmarks against the time when staff switches out your computer unexpectedly.

URLs at your fingertips. Your infrequently used sites are also organized on Delicious.com so they are easy to retrieve: for example, the menu might include an animated online tutorial for sign language, how to cut a five-point star or six-point snowflake, a refresher on Big6, or your father's recipe for black-bottom coconut pie. Have two accounts (one for school and one personal) or merge them (if librarians are always asking for your pie recipe). A valuable feature is that you can share your favorites with librarian colleagues for your mutual enrichment, a variation on the social networking site.

If you are a librarian who frequently gives workshops or even one who speaks up at various meetings, it is very helpful to know that your most valuable or elusive URLs are at your fingertips regardless of whose computer you are using or where.

Stretch for a scholarship. Self-deprecation is common: many people think they cannot possibly qualify for a scholarship. The key is tailoring your qualifications to a specific scholarship. Look for obscure possibilities that are open to a limited number of people. Capitalize on any group identity you have: ethnic, racial, religious, sons of miners, daughters of railroad personnel, single dads with disabled children. Put your reference fact-finding experience to work. Consult a counselor, but never pay money.

When applying for a scholarship, little things matter. Follow the directions to the letter. Ask a friend or colleague to review your application and incorporate those improvements. Clearly define your reasons for seeking the scholarship and your *immediate* educational goals, but not distant future ones.

Utilize free publicity. Look at national, regional, and local scholarships and take advantage of free publicity when you win one. This is not about bragging: it is about creating your brand.

Distance learning. Many colleges are now offering distance learning opportunities for adults who want to complete an interrupted education. Pursue courses at home with only an occasional visit to an actual campus. These courses may also qualify for scholarships. Put together a package that shows who you are, what challenges you have overcome, and what it would take to reach your immediate professional goal. Submit this package to the college's financial services office and to your local service clubs, auxiliaries, and lodges.

Portfolio building for you and your students. Keep a file folder on both your home and work computers with sections for all of the previously mentioned information. When it is time for a performance review or to generate a new résumé, all the information will be in one place, easy to print out. This type of portfolio building shows any current or future employer that you are serious about developing as a professional. It will also prepare you to help your students/patrons build their performance-based portfolios, which are rapidly replacing or supplementing standard report cards.

No one is too young or too old to pursue lifetime education. Experienced librarians need to constantly upgrade skills to stay competitive in a downturn. Young, unemployed recent graduates can assiduously log and document their volunteer activities to supplement their résumés.

Teach something. Everyone knows something. Perhaps you can cut out giant letters of the whole alphabet in six minutes. That is a handy skill to pass on to other teachers, librarians, or para-educators. Do not hide your light under a bushel. Volunteer to share knowledge with other colleagues. In your years of experience, have you developed some cataloging shortcuts? Can you create a podcast? As a novice fresh out of school, do you have knack for blogging or Youtube that you could communicate? Never be miserly with information that could enrich other people, but always be humble and tactful in offering it. Schedule a skill-sharing session for a district library meeting.

Educational service districts. Each state or province has different rules for how clock hours or educational units are awarded and what constitutes an awarding body. If your state uses educational service districts (ESD), which serve multiple counties, those districts often can offer off-site classes for credit (*off-site* meaning away from the ESD campus). Inquire if your school has anyone qualified to teach such an off-site course at your facility. For example, many librarians need to use Excel or a similar spreadsheet program. If there is enough interest, it may be worthwhile to have one of your school's own experts teach an Excel class to certified and classified staff. Clock hours from this class might accrue toward various certifications. Creating a library or classroom Web page with links is another possible class.

Reduce travel expenses. Having an onsite (or at least in-district) class solves problems of travel expense and travel time. Tuition may be far less than for a regular

ESD course. Local courses reduce your carbon footprint! If you could teach such a course, think about how it could build up and equip people who are struggling. Most courses take a minimum number of participants to be financially viable: quiz nearby library specialists to see if they might attend the course.

Free classes at local libraries. Many local libraries offer free, noncredit classes designed to familiarize patrons with computers, genealogy resources, and databases. Particularly if you are a para-educator or library clerk, take advantage of these and compile a list of all classes taken.

If you are mentoring someone trying to enter the workplace, share these low-cost educational options as a guideline.

Camp out. Your state or provincial library may be hundreds of miles away, but if it offers attractive free workshops, combine a weekend camping trip with course time. Consider an overnight stay with friends or family to advance your educational goals.

Audit! Some library workers do not need degrees: auditing courses may cost less.

Lifestyle classes. Community colleges often offer less expensive *lifestyle* classes aimed more at improving quality of life rather than providing professional training. However, some lifestyle classes such as Photoshop are useful for librarians. Take advantage of the reduced fee.

Look professional. Free guidance abounds on looking professional. High-end department stores often have a consultant who will make useful wardrobe suggestions for men or women. Then take the list to a charity or consignment clothing shop. If you are just getting into the workplace, some communities have a program that matches gently used suits, jackets, briefcases, and shoes with job seekers. If you have spare professional clothing that you need to purge from a closet, share it via this type of service. Such programs sometimes offer free office etiquette training and advice for hair, posture, and makeup as well.

CHAPTER 4

Volunteers

 Trial period for volunteers. Before soliciting volunteers, it is essential to ask yourself one question: "How comfortable am I with strange strangers?" That is not a redundant term. Unknown volunteers are strangers who may be very strange indeed. It is useful to specify a trial period of one hour per week. The script would read, "Let's try an hour per week for a while and see how that goes." If the person turns out to be a jewel, more hours are an option. If the person is a clunker, then one hour per week is bearable with no hurt feelings.

This trial period also helps retain volunteers who may rashly want to promise three hours per week. When the flu bug, soccer tournament, and visiting relatives rob them of the three hours they promised you, they are likely to withdraw from volunteering altogether because they feel guilty for not showing up.

 Guidelines for volunteers. Another pre-solicitation task is to write volunteer staff guidelines such as the following list. The great thing about this list is that it is proactive. Instead of having extremely uncomfortable discussions about halitosis or louse infestation, handle these topics generically by going over the list aloud before the first volunteer session.

The script for this is mildly disingenuous. For parents, you can say, "I have this list mostly for the kids, but it does not hurt to go over it." Tell kids the list is for the parents. That way no one feels targeted. Personalize the list to reflect your own boundaries.

Volunteer Staff Guidelines

Please always check in at the office before proceeding to the library.

Our mission is to connect every student with information. When you help with clerical jobs, you free up our librarian to work with students.*

If the librarian is busy when you enter, check the job board.

There are usually items to shelve, shelves to straighten, and counters to wash if the job board is empty.

Please do not speak on cell phones while in the library.

Please always allow enough time to put away supplies after a job is finished.

We have many students with allergies. Please avoid wearing clothing exposed to cigarette or cigar smoke, heavy fragrances, perfumes, antiperspirants, or other potential allergens such as peanuts.

Antibacterial soap (to protect you from school germs) and mouthwash are near the job board.

*This explanation helps workers to focus on the clerical without being drawn into student conversations or searches for which they are not well prepared.

 Mentor an intern. Volunteers are not a homogenous group. Spread the net broadly. Contact local colleges, tech schools, or universities to see if student interns need placements. Identify yourself as a competent mentor. List your qualifications in the letterhead inquiry you send to the appropriate department.

 Brainstorm new sources of volunteers. Volunteer sources change over time. Be flexible.

 Homeschoolers as library pages. Let homeschoolers know that you welcome them in your library both as legal patrons and as volunteers. This could be as easy as sending a note to a local homeschooling cooperative. Homeschool parents have more discretion in the types of electives they can offer their children. The position of library aide ranks high in student popularity, even if not offered at your school. Some states have a school/home partnership, which allows districts with plummeting enrollment or budgets to connect with lucrative and educationally beneficial relationships with homeschooled students.

 Senior projects. Do not neglect students needing community service hours for senior projects. Advertise (free) in the high school newspaper for helpers. Clue in counselors and teachers. When describing the allure of library work, use the wiles of a cruise ship recruiter.

 A clipboard is your best friend. In a school of 500 students, a parent night volunteer sign-up might generate half a dozen names, especially in a junior or senior high. Instead, whenever there is a large group of students in the library, send around a clipboard with three columns: student full name, parent full name, and regular or cell phone number. Tell students they are nominating their parent for a specific job such as bringing treats. Even the youngest students know if they have working parents or if parents are unlikely to volunteer. The success rate of this type of list is very high. The phone script reads: "Hi, Brett (or Mr. Vernon if you are a more formal person), this is the librarian from _____. Alex says you might be willing to bring energy bars for our Readathon on Friday the 13th or Friday the 20th." Choose something that can be purchased (instead of homemade) to accommodate working parents. Some parents may still prefer the less expensive option of baking mini-muffins or cupcakes.

 Keep your solicitations gender free. Stay-at-home dads, stepdads, or retired uncles are great candidates for volunteer jobs. Schools are usually trying to increase the ratio of students to adult males, especially at the elementary level.

 Grandparents of both genders are underutilized. The clipboard can be sent around to garner grandparent power. Script: "Hi, Mrs. Solvang, your grandson Rafael thought you might be willing to help us stick on some barcodes at his school library. Could you help us for an hour this Thursday or Friday?"

Some librarians are terrified of making phone sales pitches. Most of the scripts provided in this book can also be delivered by e-mail, texting, or postcards. Students often like to do this type of phone call with a script.

 Ask for something easy. Sweet reasonableness is the hallmark of the successful solicitor. Give a choice of two dates or times. Do not leave the date nebulous. Script: "Okay, I have you down for Tuesday, the 7th, at 1:30. Does that sound right? Would you like an e-mail reminder? What is your e-mail address?"

Juvenile offenders. Juvenile offenders often need to work off community service hours. With the collaboration of your administration, offer the library as a possible work site. Large muscle jobs such as shifting books and mechanical jobs like working with the photocopier may be a good fit for these youngsters *from your own school*. Avoid database jobs where hacking is a possibility.

In-house suspensions. With administrative permission, recruit an otherwise capable student who might be spending time separated from his or her class.

Scout projects. Contact the local scouting office to identify Boy Scout, Girl Scout, Mariner and Sea Scout honors aspirants who need a hefty project to complete for the community. For example, a youth trying for Eagle scout rank may relish your request for new library counters and supply both the materials and the manpower.

 Volunteerism is growing in the United States and Canada. Ask a local small group (perhaps from a synagogue, church, or temple) to meet you at the library on a Saturday or Sunday to do a one-time job that has been weighing on you and that could benefit from adult hands and minds. Since they have already set aside this time for their meeting, they are available. Ahead of time, prepare well with sufficient supplies and tools.

 Off-site volunteers can be stellar performers. Many people are not available to help during library hours. Create portable jobs to do at home. Some samples of home jobs would include attaching Mylar covers to book jackets or applying heavy-duty vinyl covers to paperbacks. Some products even have a how-to DVD. A dozen books and supplies fit easily into cardboard box or reusable plastic crate for light-weight transport. Ask the volunteer to pick up the crate.

Retirees. Assisted-living facilities or retirement homes are another possibility for work parties. The type of ongoing cooperation promoted on the library campus can extend to the community. If the library receives donated books or other materials not suitable for its clientele, pass these on to a local rest home library. Some senior citizens enjoy racy books, political commentary, and classics so do not prejudge their breadth of interests.

Projects for assisted living homes. While delivering the free books, contact one or more residents via their activity director to help with a long-term library project. It is best to choose a job to repeat at intervals rather than a variety of different jobs. Cleaning, mending, and erasing pencil marks from books is one job possibility. Electric erasers are easier for people with limited hand strength to use. Elders can use baby wipes or antibacterial wipes to sanitize book covers. Shut-ins can hand address envelopes for overdue letters. To reciprocate, whenever you have an opportunity to obtain a free or 25-cent large print book or an adult audiobook, save it as a contribution to the residents' library.

Photograph residents. The amount of volunteer help received from a rest home does not always match the librarian's investment of time, but the dignity of being useful and the extension of more reading opportunities for residents make this a good tradeoff. Photograph assisted-living residents working on your school's books and use the photos on the library Web site to promote a transgenerational community. Librarians need to model civic service too.

Phone messages via volunteers. Some library systems rely on e-mail to deliver overdue notices without the cost of postage and with minimal staff time. Not all libraries have this luxury, especially in communities where patrons do not have readily available Internet access or even electricity. Phoned overdue messages are useful. Here are two simple ways to do phone messages with volunteers.

Phone themselves. Method 1: Ask students with overdue items if they have voice mail or an answering machine at home. Let the students call home on the library phone to leave themselves a message to return materials. Students often find this riotously funny.

Phone other people's parents. Method 2: Ask a reliable student to use a script to advise a number of parents/guardians about overdue materials. The student voice is very nonthreatening compared to that of an adult. Most daytime calls will go to an answering machine anyway. To maintain student privacy, the list will not include the titles of any books.

> Sample script: "Hello, I am a student helper from X library letting you know that
> _____ has two library books that were due on _____. Your student
> knows or can find out the titles. Please return the items right away. Thank you."

Train the student helper to hand the phone to the librarian immediately if any caller is impolite. (This training is unlikely to ever be used.)

Phone reminders in other languages. For parents who do not speak English (English or French in Canada), employ a student helper who shares their language to make the calls using the preceding script translated into that language. Here is a sample of a Spanish language script. Keep in mind that many people from Mexico and other Central American countries do not speak Spanish as their primary language. They may speak a tribal language.

(Yo no hablo Español pero) según nuestra lista, su estudiante tiene un libro u otros materiales prestados de la biblioteca. El tiempo de préstamo se ha vencido.

Por favor de entregarlo tan pronto posible. Si se ha perdido por favor de pagar la cantidad indicada para reemplazarlo. Si paga con cheque, se dirige a _____. Gracias por su atención.

(I do not speak Spanish but) our records show that your student has an overdue book or other materials. Please return it to the library right away. If the item is lost, please pay the amount indicated (the cost of replacement). If you are paying with a check, make it out to _____. Thank you for attending to this matter.

 Recruit retired teachers or librarians as volunteers. Many communities have organizations specifically for retirees such as AARP or AAUW (American Association of University Women). Woo members of these groups.

 How many volunteers does it take to replace a librarian? This is not the opening line to an old joke. Around the country as an economy measure, library clerks are replacing trained librarians who have master's degrees. The next step is to replace the clerk/specialists with free volunteers. Reserve some skills to yourself in the interests of preserving your job.

 Reward volunteers generously with words. A free online poetry dictionary is an efficient tool to create 10 lines of gratitude in 10 minutes. Find 10 words that rhyme with the volunteer's first or last name: Marlene, clean, teen, scene, queen, seen, serene, magazine. The doggerel thank you almost writes itself. Typing it up in a font such as Juice on colored paper creates a keepsake.

 Photo memory. Create a photo thank you with the volunteer as the centerpiece. Print these out or, better yet, post them on the library Web site. For child volunteers whose faces cannot be on a Web site, photograph the backs of their heads or allow them to hold a favorite book to partially conceal their faces.

 A one-size thank you does not fit all. Most volunteers fall into one of two camps: people who like being praised or recognized publicly and people who loathe it.

 Do not regift. Avoid anything that looks as though it has already made the rounds: bedraggled boxes, bent corners, multiple mark down stickers laboriously scraped off, impersonal fragrances. A good volunteer is worth a good gift. A make-do gift is worse than no gift.

Do not spend your own money on volunteer gifts. The exception would be in rare instances when a volunteer has been astoundingly useful or saved your sanity.

Sources of Free Rewards or Gifts

Fill out a brief phone or online survey that promises a reward such as a coupon for a free dessert pizza offered by pizza chains.

Collect the free items in "Buy One, Get One Free" promotions.

Whenever you see a radio station remote broadcast booth at a shopping center, fair or home show, show your business card or library ID badge, and ask for a free T-shirt.

Using your volunteers' own birth dates, sign them up for a free birthday meal or ice cream treat at national chains that offer this amenity.

Ask for billed caps at fair booths or industry shows.

Businesses sometimes offer coffeehouse gift cards or vouchers for candy as inducements to customers.

Fast food restaurants occasionally give an incentive such as a free deluxe burger for buying a reloadable payment card. Ask them to put the free burger credit on a separate reloadable card to give as a thank you.

 Buy items that promise to be free after rebate. Then keep accurate records. Photocopy your rebate form and barcodes. The main difficulty with rebates is that you have to spend your own money up front and wait perhaps two months for the rebate check to reimburse you sometimes with follow-up letters or e-mails. (In addition to providing gifts for volunteers, back-to-school sales often offer rebate items that may help stock your own depleted supplies of specialty markers, memory sticks, and pens.)

 Free library-themed cards. Jobbing representatives such as Follett often provide attractive blank greeting cards with a library or reading theme that are excellent for a simple but heartfelt handwritten thank you.

 Cafeteria lunches. Ask your administration for several cafeteria lunches to award over the course of the year. Because of government regulations, the cooks may not be able to give away cafeteria food without going through the chain of command. For an elementary school, have kids decorate a special chair or make a crown. At a high school, a helium balloon marks the spot. Look at the menu ahead of time and choose a yummy day at the cafeteria (possible oxymoron at your school). Remember that some adults are terrified of even walking in the halls with older students. Use this reward for a gregarious volunteer.

Candy bar puns are a cheap and quick thank you combined with a sticky note.

Your help is worth 100 Grand!

I am such a Butterfingers. Thanks for your help with the labels.

You are so Special. (Hershey Dark Chocolate)

Thank you for helping me with Mounds of shelving.

Sorry, there is no PayDay for great volunteers like you.

You are a Treasure!

ID lanyards. Collect ID lanyards from conferences that your colleagues attend. Replace their nametag with your own volunteers' names typed on brightly colored paper. This also helps students address adults by name. Substitute "Valued Volunteer" to create a generic lanyard. These ID lanyards are also popular with student volunteers and have the advantage of being free instead of something ordered from a catalog. For students, use trendy designs such as those found in teen clothing store ads or lively scrapbook paper.

Keep a spiral bound notebook for volunteers. Have them jot down their name and contact information including phone, e-mail, and street address on their first volunteer day. It is embarrassing to have a volunteer return and not be able to greet and thank him or her by name. Similarly, expedite thank you notes with the address info. The notebook works better than an address book because the most current volunteers are on the most recent page.

Worksheets. Invest an hour to create a descriptive worksheet for a job that continually needs doing. Lay out the work in a logical sequence; put the tools to complete the job in one container or on one desk. Include samples of what the finished job should look like. Add a reminder to leave time at the end to put away all materials and tools.

For example, you may explain how to add reading levels to peel and stick dots inside book covers or how to laminate a paperback. By creating the worksheet, you lessen the time needed for how-to lessons. Even if you are busy with a class, you can direct the volunteer via the worksheet. Focus on creating one worksheet at a time and do not laminate until a volunteer has tried out the instructions to determine if there are any missing or unclear steps.

CHAPTER 5

Solicit Free Items: Develop as a Scrounge

Ink cartridges. In olden days, a railroad spike was worth a nickel. Youngsters would take them to a local store and swap one for a candy bar. For librarians the candy shop is currently accepting ink cartridges. Three of the major office supply chains accept certain brands of used cartridges and issue a quarterly voucher or credit reward for each one brought in. If each one is worth several dollars (and that could change instantly if technology changes), the librarian needs to be a cartridge magnet. Friends, colleagues, associates, and handball buddies should see the librarian coming and feel an immediate need to donate a cartridge. Many people do not wish to be bothered with recycling but are happy to save and even collect cartridges for such a good cause.

Free camera memory card. When the credit reward arrives in the mail, it is equal to cash that can be spent in that store. For example, a Shoestring Library probably cannot afford its own camera. With your first reward, purchase a dedicated memory card that fits your own camera but that is only used for school pictures. Then with the second batch of reward credit, purchase a multiple card reader that will transfer photos to any school computer. This allows you to publish photos to the Web and to create wallpaper of student library activities and book recommendations on any computer.

Book fairs. The two best sources for free books come from your own campus. First, encourage book fairs. These generate an immense increase in the number of age-appropriate books in your immediate community. If you are a winsome and helpful supporter (putting up posters, staffing the cash register for an hour, or directing your students in stocking the shelves), the book fair organizers may decide to let you spend some of their book credits. Whether you view this as karma, expediency, or craftiness, it still may result in a nice pile of brand new books for the library.

Bookstore bookfairs. If no volunteers are available, investigate whether a local or national chain bookstore could have a bookfair on your campus. Sometimes chains handle all the staffing and details.

Bookfair followed by book lottery. Next, all those book fair books are read once. Maybe. After a decent interval has passed, try to corral these practically new books for the library by using the lottery device described in chapter 8. The combination of the book fair followed by the lottery is essential. If students do not have books to donate, the lottery does not work.

Request a specific author. Most schools communicate with parents on a weekly basis via a printed or Internet-posted newsletter. Rather than asking vaguely for used book donations, each week specify a different author: Dr. Seuss, John Grisham, Will Hobbs, or one character: Garfield, Buffy, Bones. People respond best to a specific request.

Book memorials. At the beginning of the school year, include a tasteful announcement on your library page and via the newsletter that describes book memorials. Let people know that each memorial book will receive a lavish custom bookplate with the name of the donor or honoree and any special information the family wishes

Figure 5.1 Memorial bookplate

including the bereaved student's name. Book plates are easy to make using the borders and text box commands in typical word processing programs. (This would be a valuable skill to share.) Enlist the newsletter editor to include your distinctive border around the newsletter announcement to give a preview of the end product. Either within your automation system or via a word document, keep track of memorial books so that at a moment's notice, visitors can be shown the books they donated.

Birthday books. Birthday books do not merely build up a library, they build up a child. Let adults know that children can donate a book on their birthday and have an inscribed bookplate attached. Keep some attractive *new-looking* books on hand for parents who cannot go shopping, and publicize this in the newsletter. Instead of the borders format used for memorials, do a quick search for copyright-free clipart related either to birthdays or to the child's interests.

Microsoft clip art library. If you are using Microsoft Word connected to the Internet, you have access to a huge library of copyright-free images by clicking on "Insert" and then choosing "Clip Art." Copy the image into a Word document, click on it to create the editing box around it and then choose size. Enlarge the image to fit the frontispiece of the book. Next use the text box, to superimpose the child's name and birth date in bold.

Another source is to look under Google or Yahoo images, explaining your method to the student as you search so that it is a teaching device as well.

Make a book donation a balloon event. Group the book, the student's quick photo, and a balloon in a conspicuous spot. Mylar balloons are easy to save and refill.

Figure 5.2   Birthday bookplate

Liberate a balloon at the end of a friend's birthday party. If possible, use it in your library while it is fresh. Otherwise, deflate it by inserting a straw and pressing gently until you remove all the helium. Store flat without creases. Sometimes the store where it was purchased will refill Mylar at no cost or for $1.

Custom peel and stick bookplates. Colored paper or parchment is good for bookplates, but also ask your local printer (such as a newspaper publisher) to donate some peel and stick sheets to the library. These make superb bookplates. Try to print up several at one time, to use the whole sheet efficiently.

Cover book plates with four-inch-wide clear library tape. Design your plates to be slightly narrower than your clear tape to create a very slick, permanent plate.

Embossed metallic bookplates. When several books have been donated, ask a scrapbooking parent to create embossed metallic bookplates. Students who have not seen the process of melting pigment will be enthralled and eager to help. A supervised electric skillet is a simple, safe way to provide heat for embossing if there is no heat gun.

Ask for business commemorative books. Consider which businesses in your county are large enough or old enough to have documented their company history in a book. This is a good lunchtime conversation starter with your colleagues. Take notes. All kinds of industries mark their milestones with commemorative books, which are an invaluable history resource for any grade level.

For example, a local aluminum plant put out a book that included pictures and stories about tribal festivities surrounding the plant's dedication. This provided an elusive primary resource about local tribal members. Request the donation of several copies of such company books.

Ask for college commemorative books. Educational institutions also do milestone books that are rich in history. Contact every secondary institution within a three-county area. As long as you are in contact, ask if they would include a free decal or pennant to display in the library to encourage students to envision college in their future.

Ask for military commemorative books. Military units often do commemorative books of specific missions such as a tour of Iraq or Afghanistan. These can be an informative supplement to your country books as well as a way to show pride in service families.

Ask celebrities for their books. Famous television personalities promote books constantly. Some of these are adult books suitable for a junior high or high school library. Whenever you hear one mentioned, send off a quick e-mail stating why this particular book would be essential for your students. When a librarian whose patron base includes more than 250 students of Hispanic heritage asked Geraldo Rivera for his recent book *HisPanic,* his representative called immediately and asked how many copies. This is free book rule number one: get enough to share if possible. Culture trains people from birth not to be pushy or greedy. A Shoestring Librarian needs to be acquisitive.

Goodwill books. Goodwill Industries sometimes has a policy of donating in kind items within their own communities, a benefit that could change at any time. Inquire whether they donate books to school libraries where you live. Some have a policy of 60 books per month at one time or 15 books per week. Sometimes it is difficult to find 60 useful books at once for library or classroom use. On the other hand, if distance is an issue, it may not be feasible to check for books every week. Usually the store requires a petitioning letter from a school administrator (to expedite, you write it, he or she can sign it) along with a tax exemption number. Then the store will set up a special account for school-related books. Inquire at other charitable thrift stores as well.

Free gift cards? Elsewhere in this book, recycling ink cartridges is mentioned as a possible source of special office equipment and supplies. Eventually even the poorest library has enough staplers, markers and kick stools. If you do not see something you urgently need at the office supply store, see if they have a kiosk that features *bookstore gift cards*. Stores vary as to whether they allow reward credit to be used to purchase gift cards that will be used at other kinds of stores, but it is worth a try.

Librarian discounts. If there are thriving independent bookstores or used bookstores, patronize them for local authors and local history. They work on a narrow profit margin but often have generous teacher discounts. What if you are not a teacher? You are an educator and probably have a school ID badge or card. Stores do not usually quibble if you have adequate identification to connect you to a verifiable local school library. Sign up for a free discount card at every local or chain bookstore in your area.

Public libraries routinely buy dozens of copies of in-demand titles. When demand tapers off, they remove excess copies. Be alert to sales of withdrawn materials. Or build a relationship with a local public librarian and ask if one free copy of withdrawn no-longer-in-demand titles could be funneled to your library. Accounting practices differ for such a transfer.

Connect with Friends of the Public Library. Members may watch for categories of books your library especially needs and give you a heads up for sales or even purchase books to donate to your library as they are sorting for book sales.

A sample book is not a free book. A sample book is a publisher's investment in your future purchases. Increasingly publishers are allowing librarians to examine sample books online. This is a great tool to reduce costly mistakes in ordering, especially for series or sets. By looking at the actual page layout, pictures, photos, and font size, librarians can make wiser choices, but sometimes holding the actual book expedites selections. When you find a book that you really want to examine, offer to pay for return shipping. This may show your sincerity and result in a sample book: generally, they will give you the book to keep and not require you to pay the shipping.

Keep track of guaranteed books. Some excellent companies guarantee their bindings. Whenever you add a new book from such a company, identify it as a guaranteed book so you will recognize it if it does not hold up. Do not pay to ship it back. Ask for return postage. The guarantee does not cover dog or toddler tooth damage.

Business cards. Business cards may seem like a luxury, and the idea of ordering 500 of them ludicrous, but they carry your professional identity in a more portable fashion than letterhead. Office supply stores sell kits that allow you to make your own for a fraction of the print shop price and in limited numbers, but even that is too expensive for a Shoestring Librarian. In a precarious economy most people cannot expect to retain the same phone number or address long enough to use up cards, so printing a few on demand from your own computer keeps you current and solvent. Be sure to include your work e-mail address. You can create a dozen cards in a word processor, print them on cardstock, and trim them yourself. A business card is the lowest item on your priority list. Look at it as a 10-minute lottery ticket for which you spend a few minutes typing for a chance to win something over the course of a year.

How to use a business card. What do you do with a business card besides drop it into a fish bowl for a free lunch drawing at some restaurant? Commercial salespeople hand theirs out with abandon. A Shoestring Librarian has to acquire the habit of reaching for a business card whenever one would normally scramble for a piece of scrap paper and pen. Here are six scenarios for giving out cards. Even then, it is rare to hand out two dozen a year.

How to Use Business Cards

1. A home improvement store has put large plastic containers on clearance with a drastic markdown. They are exactly the color you need for your library. Describe the item on the back of your business card and give it to the manager of that department with your cheery request that he think of you when they get down to the last few containers.

2. A movie theater, playhouse, or museum is nearing the end of a run. Produce your card and ask to be kept in mind for a specific poster or free-standing figure that has a tie in to a popular library book. Frequently you can tape your card to the back of the item for a future phone call.

3. At a thrift store, you see some large book supports that would be perfect for your reference books. Seek out the person in charge and ask if they would consider a gift in kind (a donation of the bookends) to your library if they do not sell in the next month or so. Most thrift stores use a code on the price tag that indicates how long the item has been on the shelf. When you point out that the item you want has been in the store for two months, you have a better chance of getting it. Turn your business card into an impromptu tax receipt for the store. "Received from Handy Andy's one pair free shelf supports for School Library." Do not include a monetary value.

4. At a county fair, a parade, or a public library book sale, you see a volunteer doing an outstanding job of creating a display or bulletin board or sorting books. Admire the work and solicit the worker, handing over your card for

future reference. You are not *poaching* volunteers. If a person is volunteering in one place, he or she may be willing to volunteer in a similar capacity for you.

5. The fifth use is the most fun: connecting with colleagues. Whenever you meet new people at conferences, conventions, or even at publisher events, exchange cards with people you hit it off with or whose work you admire. If you give a workshop, be ready to hand your card to people who might want to contact you for future engagements. When you get back to your library, file the cards in your rolodex. Alternatively, add them to your computer address book if you have a business card scanner or enter them by hand.

6. Then there is always that fishbowl. Drop your business card into any restaurant drawing with the intent of winning a free meal for one of your volunteers. Let the manager know that is your goal and you may get a coupon or reduced price certificate on the spot.

Requesting reward items from nearby towns. Rural or inner-city patrons may not travel far to use rewards. Free slushies, free giant pretzels, and DVD rentals may languish unclaimed if they are not near your library. To students, give the prize itself, not the gift certificate. Adult volunteers may be able to travel for rewards.

Dumpster diving does not require hanging out in alleys. (Unhygienic and sadly unprofessional.) However, stores frequently toss items into collection bins *inside* the store, which will either go to a donation or discard site. Plants fall into this category. Flash your business card and ask if you can have them for your school. Bedding plants that are no longer in bloom may enjoy a resurrection outside the library windows. Seasonal items, especially candies, decorations, and temporary tattoos end up in markdown carts a week after the holiday. Ask for some as school rewards just before the goodies exit the store. Timing takes a bit of luck: morning of day five may see a markdown of 75 percent while by evening all things holiday vanish for new products.

For example, wrapped Christmas candies are often red and green. After purchasing, ask a student helper to sort candies into piles of red for Valentine's Day and green for St. Patrick's Day.

Is online scrounging worth it? Multitudes of sites promise freebies. A Shoestring Librarian does not have time to investigate free items that are available to millions of Internet surfers in single quantities. Free local items, yes. Free Internet items, no. If you have an avid Internet volunteer, perhaps an adult with limited mobility, this can be a satisfying treasure hunt for them, but not for you.

Be childlike. There is always one child that straggles out the last day of school with arms loaded with loot that others have left in the hallways and waste bins. Be that child.

Craft a reputation. Having a reputation as a scrounge can put you in line for many fortuitous windfalls. People automatically think of you when there is something to give away.

Two problems occur with this. First, it can make your school district look cheap or ineffectual. "What do they do with all that levy money? Why is their librarian camped out at the Thrift Store? Why don't they buy books for the schools instead of . . .?" Your frugality should not reflect poorly on your administration. *Discrete* penny pinching protects your school's standing as a district that spends voters' money wisely.

Be selective. The second problem with being identified as a scrounge is that people try to palm things off on you: resist overstuffed chairs, couches, ancient kitchen tables, and any items obviously designed for a home rather than a school. Well-meaning souls will present you with artworks of every description. To be tactful, try this script: "Wow, a two-foot tall chartreuse plastic cat. That is unique! We will use that to promote our sci-fi collection next month. *Do you want it back when we are finished or should I pass it on?*" If you think about it, there is always a tie-in to some subject area of your collection to match any atrocity. By spelling out at the beginning that it is a temporary treasure, hurt feelings are less likely. "People before things" is a great motto.

Solicit Free Magazines

Fewer weekly news magazines. Multiple weekly newsmagazine subscriptions could bury a Shoestring Librarian. Where would she find the time to enter them under serials, follow up if issues were missing, place them in binders she probably cannot afford? While the absence of subscriptions is a mixed blessing, the absence of the magazines is not a blessing at all. Students can be attracted to magazines for the same reasons adults are: graphic pictures, short amounts of text, and popular subjects.

Treat magazines as expendable. Do not inventory them or give them barcodes, or reinforcement tape. Do not pay for them. When you invest absolutely nothing in the magazine, it becomes a reading bonanza. (Do take the time to property stamp or write "Library" in bold ink to minimize theft.) The simplest way to acquire magazines is to ask people to donate a pile when they are ready to recycle them. Every few months list a specific magazine in the school newsletter. Request motorcycle magazines, animal and nature magazines, tropical fish magazines, or even one weekly news magazine and watch the donations pile up.

Aim for a colorful magazine collection. Instead of worrying about creating a balanced magazine collection, aim for a colorful one where the library tables disappear under a carpet of slick pages whenever classes visit. If you have ever managed a library with a strong collection, did students leave news magazines or science magazines on the tables? No, not as often as popular magazines. Marginal readers may be enticed by sports and truck magazines, yet librarians persist in buying instructive magazines that no one uses. A Shoestring Library does not have that luxury.

Tone it down. Truck magazines are particularly blatant in featuring lots of female skin. Librarians are champions of noncensored reading, but do not hesitate to rip out an outrageous page. For covers, use a black marker to turn a thong into shorts in under 10 seconds. This is not about going through the magazine page by page, but just eliminating one or two full-page elements that might offend parents of younger readers or alarm administrators.

Some schools have magazine sales to raise student body funds. Make a brief list of 5 to 10 magazines that the library could use. Post the list prominently near the school's front doors, on the school and library Web site, and in the newsletter. The sales company usually awards prizes. If you were going to order magazines for your home or for gifts anyway, time your purchases to achieve the most prizes (to use in the library).

Thank you note for a subscription. If a relative or friend of a student donates a subscription via a magazine drive, immediately send a real, live, paper thank-you note.

Redeem airline miles. Redeem airline miles for magazine subscriptions if the opportunity arises and let colleagues know that you would welcome their spare miles. These are not usually children's magazines but often will include news, sports, or celebrity periodicals suitable for ages 12 and up. If students do not reach for these magazines, put them in the faculty lounge for teachers When finished with your free magazines, donate them to the public library for their sales.

Buy used magazines. Visit the used magazine sale section of your public library for 10-cent copies of timeless selections such as Zoobooks. Garage sales are also a good source. Before buying, give used magazines the sniff test. Depending on where and how they have been stored, they may not be healthy purchases. Some people suggest putting books or magazines in plastic garbage bags filled with kitty litter to remove odors, but do you really want your students handling magazines that were bad enough to merit this treatment?

Free newspapers. Newspapers in Education (NIE) has suffered a terrible blow as newspapers are failing. If you are fortunate to live in an area with a thriving paper, inquire if they belong to NIE. NIE arranges for some schools to receive free classroom/library subscriptions based on corporate sponsorship and the use of undelivered vacation newspapers. Every library and school can profit from having newspapers to post, cut up, and share.

Catalogs are an overlooked free periodical. Students love poring over motorcycle, snowboard, and snowmobile catalogs, which frequently show up in public library free bins. Many states have fact-filled free horse resource brochures near grocery store exits often in the same rack as the free real estate brochures.

CHAPTER 6

Prepare for Subs and for Emergencies

 Emergency drills. Most school libraries have emergency drills connected with regular state- or province-required disaster or danger situations. Usually the school district only supplies a clipboard and loud bells. Knowing that as many as 30 children or young adults may need guidance and care makes it sensible to have more tools at hand than a clipboard. Public and collegiate libraries generally have fewer drills but still need to prepare for emergencies.

 Familiarize yourself thoroughly with your building's emergency plan. When school library doors remain open for easy access, use the key to keep them in the locked mode in case of a lockdown necessitated by a terrorist or criminal act. Take the following list to your next district library meeting and brainstorm answers.

 Flip chart or poster. Most librarians act sensibly in emergencies, but often multiple courses of action are possible, with a district preferring a specific response. Ask whether your district has, or could compile, a flip chart of emergency guidelines. Having a chart or poster reduces the expense of staff training time. For example, see the next hint.

 Prefer to refer. Most school districts prefer to have all staff refer media (TV, radio, Internet, and newspaper) reporters to the administrative office in the event of an emergency rather than giving statements on their own. As librarian you may already know this, but do the many people who sub for you know it? Go over all the information in this chapter with your sub or at a minimum print it out for your sub.

Know What to Do!

Does your district have a protocol for dealing with specific emergencies?

A student collapses in the library and begins to convulse . . .

A shouting, incoherent stranger bursts through the library doors . . .

The room begins to shake, with books falling to the floor . . .

Water begins to flow through the door and under baseboards . . .

A window shatters, with glass flying in all directions . . .

A teacher gasps for breath after an insect sting . . .

A newspaper reporter calls to ask about a rumored bomb threat . . .

A para-educator has a sudden asthma attack . . .

The lights go out and computers flicker . . .

Flames appear blocking the library exit . . .

A student brandishes a weapon . . .

 Never assume student blood is harmless. Latex gloves are essential to have in the emergency cupboard. Obtain several pairs from the school nurse and keep them in a clear plastic container with a lid, such as the kind that deli meats come in. The red-lidded ones are especially easy to see.

 Bring an old blanket or throw from home for first aid. Keep it clean in a sealed plastic bag next to the glove container.

Know who is at risk. Inside the emergency cupboard door, away from public view, post pictures of students who have allergies or medical conditions along with the instructions for their care should need arise. The school nurse generally sends this confidential information. Hang a piece of paper over it so you can flip up the page to see the info quickly.

 Keep a windup flashlight at the back of the keyboard drawer. This type of light does not depend on batteries. Windup flashlights frequently are available as prizes or loss leaders. Books Are Fun periodically features these flashlights. Several different companies visit schools with displays of books and gift items at greatly reduced prices.

Besides their visits being convenient, these companies frequently give one book to the library for every 10 items ordered by staff. Libraries can accumulate binoculars, books, flashlights, and other items. If no company is currently coming to your campus, ask your administrator if you can invite one.

 Free batteries at drugstore. A possible source of free AA batteries for flashlights or audio-visual remotes in the library is the local film processing counter at a drugstore. Stores are required to remove the single battery from disposable cameras before dealing with the film. Some stores keep these barely used batteries in a container for disposal. Ask if your library can reuse them instead. This keeps them out of the landfill and saves the library money at the same time.

A windup lantern is available via outdoor stores. Several minutes of winding obtain an hour of energy. The lantern has roughly five times the illuminating power of the flashlight because there are five LED bulbs. This lantern is most necessary in extreme climates faced with blizzards or hurricanes, coupled with the supervision of larger groups of children. Raise the lantern to a high spot in the room to cast the most light. One possible way to acquire a lantern is to purchase one (saving the receipt so it can be returned if necessary) and then to display it along with its cost at a Parent Teacher meeting. It is a modest request.

Label a flyswatter. A flyswatter, or wasp swatter, is an inexpensive purchase that can protect patrons. In its absence, a flip-flop sandal or folded newspaper makes an adequate swatter. Avoid any spray products. Contact your custodian if the problem persists.

Suck it up. Any vacuum with a hose and nozzle can also double as a pest trap to suck up spiders, yellow jackets, bees, and hornets unless your school has a resident bee whisperer. Usually contact the custodian to take larger creatures such as frogs, toads, and snakes outside unless there is an immediate threat to students. In that event, evacuate the students.

No peeking! Without looking around, can you accurately state where the library fire extinguisher is? Make sure you know its location. Take it down occasionally to refresh your memory as to how the wall clasps work and how to activate it. The time for practice is before the blaze. When a wastebasket fills the room with smoke and flames shoot six feet in the air from a cherry bomb or torched papers, the temptation is to turn the container over to smother the fire immediately. This can result in burned hands, singed eyebrows, and melted carpet. Habit will help you reach automatically for the extinguisher. Put it on the map or the instructions that you leave for your sub.

Fire department demonstrations. Fire departments sometimes offer free fire extinguisher demonstrations and practices. Contact them about doing a skill-sharing session as your contribution to a faculty meeting.

List storm instructions. Include where the rain covers are stored for computers, how to manage the surge protector, and safety precautions unique to your climate.

Label the phone handset. Either or both of these phrases should be taped to the handset of your phone. *In case of emergency, dial 911 or the office _____. Answer the phone by saying, "Library, student speaking."* The first thing emergency responders may ask is the phone number and the address so those should both be visible on or near the phone as well. In old buildings, phones may have lost all identifying features. Replace missing information so that students, adult patrons, or subs can operate efficiently.

Equip Substitutes

District protocols. First of all, acquaint the sub with the district protocols for dealing with emergencies as detailed in the first part of this chapter.

Print out directions. Make a print resource available for substitute librarians in your absence. Compile a binder with the most common problems and emergencies that a sub will face including logging into both the computer and the library, pulling up class rosters and handling safety drills and weather-related difficulties.

Screen captures or grabs. The simplest way to achieve this is with screen captures. Before you begin, clear your monitor of all open applications to eliminate distracting backgrounds. (Windows operating system lets you couple PrtSc with the Alt key to capture only the active window.) To create a screen capture, bring your library program "Log In" dialog box up to the upper left corner of the computer screen. (You are just capturing the picture, not your actual password.) These are just like the error screen captures that were discussed previously. Next, open a word processing document that you name "Sub Instructions" and press "paste." The Log In you captured should appear.

Paste in more screen captures to illustrate the steps needed to check books in and out, take roll, and demonstrate evacuation routes. Use a highlighter or red marker to identify salient points. Put all the printed and captioned screen captures into plastic sleeves in a binder or laminate them for your sub. Screen images sometimes stay valid for several years before needing updates. These visual cues are a tremendous help in supplementing written directions. A Shoestring Librarian does not have time allotted to train a sub.

Have a set of clipboards primarily for subs. (You can also use them when the computer is down or when you are called away from the circulation desk or have to receive phone calls.) The clipboard should have a minimum of 15 pages for orderly checkouts in the event the sub lacks computer skills. Each sheet will hold about 20 transactions. Having two or three clipboards available at one time speeds checkouts for a whole class. Any librarian who has ever returned to work after an illness only to confront flurries of sticky notes and scraps of binder paper with incomplete checkout info knows the comfort of having a form that requires students to list their student number, first and last names, book or media title, and barcode. A printed spreadsheet is the easiest way to enclose this info in boxes instead of letting it straggle in illegible lines down the page. Upon return to work, immediately transfer the info to the computer so you do not miss any transactions. (This is another great skill-sharing moment with the added advantage that the form itself can be e-mailed to other librarians, printed in volume, or stored in Delicious.com.) You will want to check older students' entries on the clipboard for accuracy while they are still present; you will also need to fill out the forms for the youngest patrons.

CHAPTER 7

Concerning Health

Add large movements. If logging and fishing top the most dangerous jobs list, librarians float gently to the bottom of that list. However, hazards still exist. Eye blinks, keystrokes, and mouse movements do not qualify as large muscle exercise. Many deskbound librarians feel tied to their nonergonomic chairs by the demands of circulation, ordering, or reference. Analyze how to add large movements to the library day.

Pony express. When teachers request library materials, deliver them. A brisk walk to their part of the building will be more than repaid in increased energy. To save time, avoid using the halls when students are passing. Time your trip so the library is not unsupervised for long.

Pedometer. The single best thing you can do for your health is to buy and wear a pedometer (she said pedantically). Keep trying to nudge up the number of steps you take per day. The added benefit of going to the student in the library instead of having the student always come to you is an increased personalization of service.

Spring-loaded return book bins are a hazard. When bending over to unload them, it is awkward to bend the knees to lift the weight of the books with the legs. One alternative is to create a counter-height book return area or to remove the wheels and elevate the bin so it can be emptied from a standing position.

Fingerless compression gloves. Check your district supply catalog for fingerless compression gloves if the library is consistently cold. As budgets plummet, so will thermostats. Not only do these gloves allow maximum fluidity in typing, but also students think they look extremely cool.

Obtain an ergonomic chair. Building administrators often order generic chairs in batches without considering the different purposes for which they will be used. A 300-pound teacher and a 100-pound teacher need different chairs. It is cheaper in the end to buy a chair that fits the user. Volunteer to pick up a chair using a purchase order. This gives you the flexibility to pick the best chair for you. Buying a chair through a catalog is about as successful as buying unknown jeans through a catalog. Try on several chairs to get the best fit.

Find a low-cost ergonomic chair. When administrators are agonizing over painful personnel cuts, a chair is a low priority. Check nearby towns or cities for used office furniture stores. As opposed to standard thrift stores, these stores specialize and are more likely to have well-designed chairs in good condition.

Search the local pages of Craigslist for an ergonomic chair.

Protect your eyes. Consult an Internet site such as that of the American Optometric Association to learn about your computer and eye health. Computer vision syndrome (CVS) is common among librarians. Even if you do not normally wear glasses, you may benefit from a computer prescription pair. Exercises can reduce headaches and eyestrain. Proper placement of the screen and its angle diminish neck and shoulder pain. Leslie Pepper in *Parade* magazine advises that the workstation monitor be five to nine inches *below* eye level. Consult your ophthalmologist for your best height and other wise practices.

Control glare. Experiment with blinds, baffles, or a foot-square portable screen to block glare on your computer screen that may occur seasonally.

Artificial tears. Consult your ophthalmologist or school nurse about using artificial tears to reduce computer eyestrain. Keep bottled tears and lens cleaners conveniently at hand.

Mold or mildew. Students and librarians alike are threatened by airborne pollutants such as dust and mold spores. Many impoverished libraries do not have vacuums with HEPA filters or else lack money to replace the filters. Custodians may give carpets a cursory once-over every few weeks. Ideally, janitors vacuum bookshelves periodically, but many understaffed buildings never manage that. If you identify mold or mildew, immediately advise a superior in writing.

Antibacterial sprays or wipes. Keeping the library clean is not the librarian's job, but keeping the environment healthy is. It is appropriate to request antibacterial wipes or surface sprays for keyboards, countertops, and phones. In many classrooms, teachers have students wash desks. Discuss with your building administrator plans for keeping library tables safe for all patrons. Your school nurse will probably distribute hand sanitizer to keep at your desk.

Gel wrist supports may help stave off carpal tunnel syndrome. Also investigate ergonomic mice or keyboards. These are good products to purchase with reward credits if your school cannot afford to buy them. A scrolling mouse reduces hand fatigue. Be sure to adjust the settings on your computer so that scrolling matches your visual/mental scanning pace. If you do not know how to do this, ask a colleague or student.

Is the surface of your computer keyboard too high? If your wrists are higher than your elbows when typing, consult your school nurse or safety officer for advice. A keyboard drawer is something you can purchase and install yourself if absolutely necessary, but even a Shoestring Library can afford this ergonomic safeguard.

Do your feet touch the ground? Everyone's feet touch the ground when standing, but do your feet touch the ground when sitting? Deep vein thrombosis or various other ailments happen when dangled legs restrict circulation. Make a footrest from materials at hand such as a brick in a flat box, a pillow or several boards nailed together. Keep an eye out for a used office footrest.

Mobile low stool. Some volunteers or librarians may find it difficult to shelve, straighten, retrieve, or inventory books on the lowest shelves. For safety and convenience, consider a low, padded library stool with swivel wheels that enables ease of movement among library stacks. Since such stools are only knee-high, equip Fido with a pet leash that will make it easy to tow anywhere in the library.

CHAPTER 8

Contests

Sponsor a book-alike contest. Periodically, pick a phenomenally popular book where patrons identify with the characters, human or not. Photograph a batch of aspiring Coralines, Hopes, Harry Potters, Gandalfs, Eeyores, or even Pokey Puppies. Post the gallery of book-alikes on a bulletin board or library Web page (keeping in mind your school's Internet safety precautions; do not include student names). If doing a hallway gallery, blow up the photos to 8 × 11 size inexpensively by using the photocopier. Let students discuss why certain patrons best match their idea of the character's appearance. Limit the contest to multiple characters in one specific book at a time. The laurel wreath of Roman fame is a sufficient prize. Circle the photo of the winner with clipart laurels. The terrific aspect of this contest is that it lets quirky students shine and costs nothing. Assemble a basket of props to help along their imaginations.

Establish a lottery. Patrons receive a lottery number for each book donated. Publicize a wish list with some high-demand books or authors earning extra numbers at your discretion. Many people are willing to give up a book after reading it once.

A lottery requires a prize that people want to win. Large stuffed animals that take two arms to carry are a hefty incentive. Purchase a used, but perfect, animal at thrift store or garage sale. Most students of any age have felt carnival envy and will welcome the chance to win. If possible, choose an animal with its spotless, unbent tags still attached. If the tag looks ratty, remove it. Immense animals that will not fit into a subcompact car often cost less than five dollars.

Figure 8.1 Stuffed animal envy

Tote the creature. To generate interest, drag out the stuffed animal whenever classes or groups visit the library. Carry the creature to the cafeteria or school assemblies and post its photo on your library Web page. Limit the lottery to six weeks or less. To minimize bookkeeping chores and the cost of tickets, number the lines in a notebook and have students enter their names once for each book donated unless it is an extra value book.

DVD lottery. If you would like to broaden or begin a DVD collection for your library, get on a list to receive some desperately awaited, book-connected DVD. Major book chains sometimes give educators a head start to purchase a voucher. Dangle the voucher as a prize to students who donate a used DVD to the DVD lottery. For the cost of one DVD, the library may receive many DVDs.

Stage a cupcake contest. Purchase cake mix and pre-made frosting on sale to create cupcakes that cost less than 10 cents each. Add one-half cup of flour to the cake mix and three extra tablespoons of water to extend it to classroom size. Fill cupcake liners only halfway. (A Shoestring Library does not have 24-cupcake classes.) Even if you have never used a pastry bag, purchase a disposable kit with throwaway bags. Insert a large star tip that comes with the bag and fill half way with icing. Twist the top of the bag shut. Do not put the icing near the edge of the cupcake: simply make a tight spiral in the middle. It will look as though it came from a bakery and have three advantages. It is faster and tidier than frosting with a knife, it costs less because less icing is used, and students get less sugar.

Create a cupcake contest entry sheet. This lists teacher, patron, book name, pages read, and a box for running class total. A spreadsheet is a quick way to do this, but word processing also works. Print up enough sheets to give teachers 10 forms each. As people finish a book, they enter the pages read and total the results. This *running total* saves the librarian time and gives the students large number addition practice (essential even in high school). Resist the request for calculators. Once a week, award cupcakes to the class with the most pages. It is amazing that even teens can be motivated with such an inexpensive reward. Refer to the volunteer chapter for hints on obtaining cupcakes without having to make them all yourself. This is a long, explicit hint included because of its phenomenal success in getting students to read thousands of pages.

Bizarre prizes need not cost money. Enlist the school office that receives packages to save bubble wrap. Cut it roughly into six-inch squares and use these to reward students who wash library tables or dust bookshelves. Students will be clamoring to be on the scrub up list. Besides standard wrap with bubbles the size of walnuts, do not ignore large format bubbles that hold a pint or more of air. Those make a satisfying, but nonthreatening kaboom. No age is too sophisticated for goofy prizes.

Forever blowing bubbles. For a perennially popular favorite, with permission of the hosts, collect leftover miniature jars of bubbles frequently given as wedding reception favors. Use these as rewards or prizes.

Figure 8.2 Bubble wrap prizes

Clothesline full of prizes. Stretch a wire or clothesline across the library and suspend clearance-priced items from your cartridge rewards for prizes. Horse-, kitten-, and dog-themed paper items as well as portfolios embellished with skulls, tattoos, and camouflage motivate students to enter their book reviews in your online contest.

The bounty hunter contest requires discretion. At the end of the school year, when all your efforts to retrieve a few stubbornly missing books have come to naught, enlist select students (none with brass knuckles) in a cheerful, nonthreatening scavenger hunt mode to contact people with overdue books. Either the borrower or the bounty hunter, or both, can return the materials for a reward such as a can of soda. Brand name pop often goes on sale for Memorial Day or Victoria Day at perhaps a quarter per can, a miniscule bounty for a $25.00 book. To protect student privacy, give the bounty hunters the overdue notice stapled shut with only the student name visible.

Enter contests yourself to win things for the library. Carry peel and stick address labels to place on entry forms at home shows, fairs, and library conventions. Address labels with your library name and address often show up in the mail unsolicited or can be obtained by making a small donation to any charity that prints them, such as the Humane Society. You can also use these labels if you have not created business cards.

Figure 8.3 Training students for acts of kindness

Some schools have an all-star award. You can create one even if your school does not. Name it anything you like. The all-star method is to have a very low-cost reward for which students compete. Whenever a student does something kind or useful for the library, hand out a brief paper form to fill out with name, grade, and a two-word description of the kindness such as "Shelving Books," "Washing Tables," or "Moving Chairs." At the end of the week, announce the winner from among all the entries. Draw or pick a name and award the prize over the intercom.

If a parent handles the awards for the whole school, display the prizes costing less than a dollar each in a central area along with photos of the current week's winners.

This pool of prizes allows all staff the simplicity of rewarding students frequently with minimal cost.

CHAPTER 9

Diversity Projects

 Diversity décor. A library has a unique opportunity to flavor a campus because, outside of the lunch room or cafeteria, it is the one room that nearly every student and teacher passes through on a regular basis. Each library is composed of the same simple elements: shelves, counter, lights, and seats. These combine to create a drab, boring, stimulating, or soothing environment. A Shoestring Librarian looks at how to bring low-cost variety in a way that has students doing a virtual twirl in the lobby because the space makes them feel good. Diversity decorating simplifies that process.

 Storage room doorways. With permission, dress up closet or storage room doorways with art such as a Chinese dragon embellished with metallic paint. Students can briefly research the difference between Chinese and Japanese dragon styles and the historic animosity between the two countries. Connect all library student art projects to the realm of classroom-based objectives or curricula.

 Free foreign-language newspapers. Newspapers or magazine pages in other languages make an interesting background for bulletin boards. Instead of using butcher paper, cover the board with sections of newsprint. The best places to pick up free papers are restaurants. Mexican restaurants are especially likely to have Spanish or bilingual newspapers. If possible, obtain two copies of the same paper to use the front and back of each page.

 Enlist teachers to aid in your search. International markets or night markets are a good place to look for Asian newspapers. Vendors may wrap produce in old papers. Ask proprietors to share some with you. Your local library may discard magazines

Figure 9.1 Doorway dragon

in Middle Eastern or European languages. Media that uses non-Western alphabets or characters especially captures student attention.

 Braille is another language to explore. Ask a visually impaired student for old magazines or contact a regional library. Staple the Braille pages up to cover the bulletin board. Since teen and children's magazines rely highly on illustrations, the Braille versions have many cultural surprises. This is a good time to see if your school is Braille labeled for restrooms and escape doors.

 A faux-Braille experience. Use a dull pencil to bump a word onto thick paper, creating a word such as "empathy" with regular letters by a series of raised dots. With the card out of sight under the table, let students try to read the brief message with their fingers. Explain that the Braille alphabet is far different. If the library has the ability to project Internet images, show a working Braille typewriter.

 Peel and stick Braille dots. An alternate way to do a Braille bulletin board is to use peel and stick dots on plain background paper: allow students (eyes closed) to read the dots with their fingers. Use the real Braille alphabet to spell out a secret message. Encourage students to solve the message by using Internet resources.

 Mexican clothing to exhibit. Mexico is a popular vacation spot for people all over the United States and Canada, so souvenirs are plentiful. Many people come back with embroidered blouses, dresses, and shawls that seldom get used. Uncomfortable, but showy, sombreros end up in attics. E-mail staff to ask if the library can borrow clothing. Run a dowel through the arms of ponchos, serapes, dresses, or shirts. Suspend the dowel with clear monofilament fishing line. Center the sombrero on the middle of the dowel using its ties. Secure monofilament line with a square knot (right over left, left over right) or with a fishing knot to create a loop.

Sikh holidays. Sikh holidays are more closely tied to their religious roots and so are a little more difficult to explore equitably at school, but newspaper restaurant ads can introduce students to that cuisine. If the community has an active Sikh culture, photos of their yearly parades and feasts may be in local newspapers or online for printing. They also participate in India's cultural holidays. Sikhs are often eager to expose communities to their practices.

Faux henna. India has many secular holidays that have evolved from formerly religious holidays, so it is easier to create displays combining saris draped from the ceiling and marigold plants when spring bedding plants go on sale. Duplicate henna decorations of hands by students using washable brown markers with their parents' permission. Photograph close-ups of their handiwork. Again, students do the research using information access skills they are learning in the library in order to find out that henna designs began as religious expressions to protect the wearers.

Asian clothing. Many people have worked in or emigrated from East Asia. With fond memories, tourists bring back Korean hanboks, Japanese kimonos, or richly embroidered Chinese garments. Borrow these from parents, students, and teachers. Instead of a dowel, hang these from a strong piece of bamboo available at garden supply stores.

Local immigrant cultures. Investigate the rich immigrant communities specific to your area such as Hmong, Cambodian, Islamic, Polish, Italian, Irish, or Mixtec. Even if there are no artifacts to display, play free online music from those cultures to broaden your students' world. Request the donation of used audio speakers to amplify your computer.

Americana. For an Americana theme, hang one or two pairs of bib overalls by their suspenders on a long handled shovel or other tool with no sharp points or edges. Fill all the pockets with farm-themed paperbacks. Suspend a Future Farmers of America (FFA) jacket or 4-H uniform in front of a bulletin board to further the theme.

Native American or First Nation regalia. Regalia, unlike the clothing mentioned previously, is often too rare for open display, but a jingle dress or sturdy Pendleton dance shawl can open discussion about modern-day tribes.

Thread a dowel through an African dashiki. For holidays such as Martin Luther King Day or observance of Black History month, dashikis, kaftans, kinta cloth hats, and other international clothing are often available in city thrift stores, but it is a question of serendipity as to finding them. Expose students to the beauty of African baskets by borrowing several to fill with related media. If you have no access to African artifacts or clothing, use "How to create an African headwrap" or other online tutorial as the library computer wallpaper for a week.

Figure 9.2 Native American jingle dress

 Borrow vivid South or Central American textiles. Travelers or groups who have volunteered for relief or building efforts there often bring back handwoven fabrics or clothing. Instead of merely displaying such clothing, wear it regardless of your own ethnicity. If no one has clothing to lend, dress in an improvised Jamaican outfit for the day's booktalks; dare to wear a headwrap! Each of these diversity projects is combined with media to match.

 Genocide. Make genocide as represented by Jewish, Kurdish, Armenian, Rwandan, Bosnian, Ukrainian and other cultures the focus of a more somber diversity display. Acquaint your students with genocides or politicides going on in our century. You may wish to wear a black armband to promote discussion. Have strips of black fabric for students to craft armbands as well, explaining that the custom refers to mourning. Instead of buying new fabric, cut up an old black garment.

 Tying curriculum to library projects. Here is an example of how a social studies classroom-based assessment (CBA) is supported by a library diversity project. (Your state or province probably has its own terminology for mandated curriculum.) Students of sixth grade geography might study the push/pull of emigration/immigration. How are inhabitants pushed out of one country and pulled or attracted to another?

Students can create paper, geometric Talavera tiles to help them view Middle Eastern Islamic culture and architecture, which avoids use of people or animal images. The byproduct of this Internet and database search for authentic tile designs is that students explore the connection of Mexico's New World Talavera pottery to Spain's Talavera and then discover Spain's North African connection during Moorish occupation as multiple push/pulls are in motion over several centuries and two hemispheres.

Over-the-top hint. Many secondary schools have kilns. Keep your eye open for new, unused, leftover tiles at garage sales. Smooth, four-inch white, grey, or beige tiles work best. Ask your school's art teacher to supply four colors of tile glaze. Have students paint their Talavera design on the tile instead of on paper. Each color

Figure 9.3   Student-designed Talavera tiles

Figure 9.4   To risk one's life for the truth

needs a minimum of four coats. Fire the tiles in the school kiln. Attach the tiles to a piece of cement board screwed onto the wall for durable, but reversible wall art. The tiles over these library doors have a quote used in a Madeline L'Engle book: *vitam impendere viro—to risk one's life for the truth.*

CHAPTER 10

Priceless Relationships and Shallow Contacts

Supporting others. Many of us barely have enough energy to see what is immediately in front of us: the next task, deadline, or obligation. We are not eager encumber ourselves with a larger vision. As librarians, we have already taken on the huge task of creating a discerning, information-literate generation. But there is an element that we need to add to an already staggering job description: widespread district and community support/promotion.

Embrace the parent-teacher association. Librarians cannot handle cash: the PTA can. Enlist the PTA to manage any cash you generate.

For example, if the PTA is having a book fair, gather up six desirable, nearly new books (from one of your scrounging efforts) and have a drawing for them. Put each batch of three books in a gallon zip lock bag. Provide a large fruit jar or coffee can with trimmed recycled paper for tickets. Tickets for the drawing are 25 cents or five for a $1 donation. The PTA collects the money donated for the tickets and awards the books to the winners at the end of the book fair. The PTA then donates the collected money to the library. For everyone concerned this is an easy and legitimate way to acquire $25 cash and to build student libraries.

COURT the PTA. What can you do to cement your relationship with the PTA so that they will want to help you? Minimum is membership. PTA membership usually costs less than $10 for one year. E-mail your colleagues to encourage them to join. Offer to collect their payment checks. Put up a poster. Send treats to a PTA meeting once. Build them up.

PTA has suffered a serious decline for a huge variety of economic reasons. Meetings often involve just a few faithful officers. Single-parent homes, parents working multiple jobs, and the demands of ferrying kids to sports teams have all affected attendance. Teachers often no longer attend, partly because fewer teachers live in the districts where they teach. An evening meeting may require a drive of 20 miles or more. Para-educators generally do not attend either (probably because they are earning so little that they do not wish to donate their evenings as well).

Ideally, regardless of whether the PTA does anything for the library, make it your mission for the library to promote the PTA. They do your school good.

Dream grants. When some money is available for books, award teachers a $150 dream grant to buy whatever they want for the library. Sometimes it is difficult to get teacher input about purchases. A dream grant delivered via a fancy font e-mail gets far more responses than a traditional query. When the books arrive, make sure respective teachers preview their dream grant books first.

A prescription for loyalty. Use Yahoo or Google images to obtain the pharmacy symbol and create a prescription form. Scribble (legibly) this message on the form: "If you are suddenly feeling ill, send your class to the library for a great database lesson or quiet, supervised recreational reading. Have them take two books and call me in the morning." Print up multiple copies and place in teachers' mailboxes during flu season.

Technology people. Another way to create the prescription is to use Microsoft Word's insert clip art function if available (as mentioned in the birthday and memorial book plate hints) but consider the following: a novice can enjoy this product immediately, but with training or experimentation, you can change the colors, sizes, orientation, and even layers of the images. This could be a time-saving technology tip so consider asking your district if they could provide it during a staff meeting. Or it could be expanded into a whole workshop. Cultivate good relationships with technology people.

Thinking of you. Greeting card companies make millions by selling thinking of you cards. Librarians can reap big rewards conveying those same thoughts via sticky notes. When you come across a magazine article or an online story that matches a colleague's interests or passions, photocopy it, tear it out, or print it out, slap on a sticky note with your regards and drop it in his or her box. This is not a chore on an endless to do list, but rather a friendly, serendipitous connection that happens occasionally.

Home, home on the range . . . Where seldom is heard a *disparaging* word, and the skies are not cloudy all day. Tactful dissent is useful, but the public interactions of the librarian and the community should be upbeat. Consistently speak well of colleagues and administration. If some of them are not commendable, be silent. A Shoestring Library cannot afford foes.

Local newspapers, radio, and TV stations. Build a chatty, first-name, e-mail relationship with a local media outlet. Some newspaper publishers run various contests and graphic serialized stories to attract educators. Others send photographers to document milestones in a school's history. Select radio stations read student poetry or stories. These free benefits add up for both parties. Media gets local interest pieces and you get positive exposure.

 Airtime. Local TV stations give air time to local events and organizations including student choir or band concerts, or advertisements for upcoming plays, tournaments, book fairs, and parades. At a minimum, get on their scrolling events calendar. While building goodwill with media is not a top priority, it is painless to reply to their e-mails, to give them feedback when they ask for community comments, and to send them high-resolution photo attachments of unique library activities (protecting student identity as appropriate). Free news bites keep the virtues of your school and students in the public eye.

Positive contacts. Unfortunately, the most common contact a librarian has with parents is negative and involves overdue or missing books. Each librarian develops a personal style for dealing with an assortment of parents. A Shoestring Librarian needs to add one more tool to that style box: a positive connection. Whenever you encounter a parent in the school hallway, at a mall, in a park, or at a parade, make the effort to connect in an upbeat way. The easiest way to talk to *students* outside of school is to avoid school topics. At the mall "What's in the bag," is a great connection starter. At the fair, "See any cute animals?" At a parade "Get lots of candy?" You are letting parent and student know that you are interested in them apart from school, that you do not view their family as a vortex that swallows library books whole with distressing regularity.

How many public librarians do you know by name? The local teen librarian, the reference librarian at the nearest branch, and the program librarian are all on your team. Reach out for their help and input as well as promoting their interests. They may be able to do booktalks or contests for which you do not have time or resources. Any librarian who can bring a clear sucker with a non-poisonous scorpion inside to beguile your boy readers is a connection to foster.

Elite librarians. Most state and provincial libraries have elite librarians available for real-time conversations conducted via Internet chat. When a thorny reference question arises especially about history, politics, agriculture, or industries, and you, along with your student researchers, cannot find the answer, seek help from one of these experienced professionals. Often they can direct you to the answer immediately or they will e-mail the information within 24 hours. Most likely hours for live chat are between 10 A.M. and 3 P.M. Closed for lunch. That corresponds well to the school day.

Maintain contact with your school librarians association. The school librarians association for your state, province, or region is your advocate even if you cannot afford to belong. Their contact person can be a source of wise advice or referral.

College librarians. Typically college librarians will not be on your list of contacts, but they may help you connect with college children's literature conferences or kid lit teachers and seminars. They may also help you link up with students in library or teacher training programs. Sometimes they can refer you to campus translators for less well-known languages.

SECTION 2

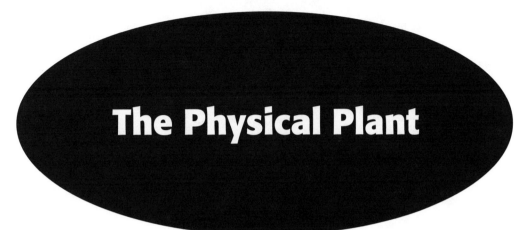

The Physical Plant

CHAPTER 11

Advice from Realtors

Take an administrator's viewpoint. Before undertaking even minor changes to the library, ask yourself the questions that administrators may ask. How long is the library space likely to remain in its current configuration? Are renovations needed or proposed for the future? Is there a district master plan? What does the rest of the school look like? How would you describe your school's style? Will your simple shoestring cosmetic changes fit into the overall look of the school?

Curb appeal. Real estate agents emphasize the importance of curb appeal. A library needs door appeal. Consult with the building custodian to determine how the entry can look its best. If the library is near an outside building door, request a walk-off mat in front of the library door so that leaves and mud will not be tracked in. If feasible, clear away any newspaper stands, recycling bins, or bulletin kiosks that obscure the entry.

Brighten the doorway. Many old buildings have grubby brass door handles and kick plates that have escaped polish for years. The custodian may not even have brass polish in the arsenal of cleaners. The royal British Navy claims that a ship is known by her brasses. Whatever material comprises the library door, enlist a student to peel off any latent tape or paper, rinse off dirt with warm water, and dry the surface. If a safe, hypoallergenic cleaner is available from the janitor, have a bucket or labeled spray bottle mixed up for an adult volunteer. Accumulated grime takes a stronger method.

Spyglass. Use an empty paper towel roll as a spyglass to examine the library. It is surprising what this simple change in viewpoint does to help analyze and troubleshoot.

 Photograph the entry. Stand at the library door and photograph the view inside. Analyze the photos for clutter, chaos, damage, or dirt. The human eye subjectively dismisses the familiar, but a photo is ruthless. Then do photo vignettes of the whole library for analysis.

 Pretend you are taller or shorter. Stand on a kickstool or kneel at floor level to view the library from the perspectives of your tallest and shortest patrons and correct any problems you observe.

 Edit the library. Over the years, successive librarians tend to add without removing. For immediate gratification, condense something to free up space or a vista.

Has your library inadvertently become a graveyard for ancient projectors? If you have to maneuver book trucks around a vintage opaque projector or unused TVs in some back room, quiz the custodian to see if these can be stored or recycled elsewhere. Also, check boxes or cabinets for unused slide projectors, filmstrip projectors, overhead projectors, and even movie projectors and obsolete or broken cassette players. Remove manual or electric typewriters.

 Evaluate old barcode scanners and audio speakers. Determine whether portable screens are still needed. Items that originally cost hundreds of dollars are sometimes difficult to consign to surplus, but editing your library is a task that pays organizational dividends. Check with your administrator for approval.

Remove stored clutter. As long as you are editing big items, be alert to small items such as stacks of floppy disks. Do your school computers even accept floppies? Perhaps there is a stash of accordion-style computer paper left over from the last century or a box of catalog cards. Streamlining your workspace by moving hidden clutter to the building surplus storage area will make you more efficient. A well-organized library contributes to your emotional health and professional efficiency.

Remove excess furniture. Tables, desks, and chairs that are taking up valuable library space may be someone else's answer to a classroom dilemma. Be sure to find out if your building inventories each room's contents. If so, you might need supervisor permission to relocate furnishings or projectors to other parts of the building.

Instead of just removing one or two pieces at a time, wait until the library is emptied of furniture for the annual floor cleaning, then, with the custodian's help, swiftly put back one item at a time until a functional (but pleasing) spareness emerges. Return any excess furniture to building storage for redistribution or sale.

 Digital photo frame. Personal art versus public art is always a real estate agent's concern. Agents suggest that your family pictures only be visible from your side of the desk and in limited numbers. The circulation desk and reference areas (sometimes the same space) need to look professional without being sterile or cold. In any library that serves youngsters, there is often a fascination with pictures of themselves doing library activities. A flip album or digital picture frame helps them to pass the time in a checkout line.

 Warm up the space with a limited number of toys. Have a few fun toys to rotate in the circulation area such as a large magnifying glass or a kaleidoscope. A collection of vintage fast food meal toys such as mini-Furbies brings out a playful nostalgia even in high school students.

Examine any plants in the library. Do they look vigorous and healthy? Is the surface soil free from any mold that might present a hazard to susceptible students?

Is fragrance absent? Are the leaves dust-free? Plants (even plastic ones) may be too labor intensive for a Shoestring Library in general. Well-cared for plants and live flowers do add to a library's ambiance and engage students. Expect flowers to be touched.

Engage Parents and Administrators

Sell the concept of the student-led library. The promotion of the library does not end with the curb appeal, ambiance, or functionality of its physical plant. You are also selling a concept to students, staff, and parents.

Inform the parents. When parents send their students to school, they do not anticipate hammers and paintbrushes in the library. Parents are not necessarily antitool; they are probook and pro–learning to read. If a parent visits an early-stage Shoestring Library with dirty, empty shelves, damaged furniture, and blank walls, suddenly a paintbrush and a book lottery seem like attractive ideas. Fortunately, the librarian who carefully communicates with parents ahead of time finds that they become advocates for the do-it-yourself, student-led library. You will find parents requesting that their students be in your classes.

Be a visionary librarian: Connect with building administrators and immediate supervisors. Formally invite the busy principal to the library when students are absent. Schedule the appointment ahead of time. You are hosting an executive meeting. Describe part A of your vision, in simple, straightforward language. (This is not the time to reveal your 10-year plan.) Prepare and share a concise, one-page description of what you want to undertake, how much it will cost, and how it will be funded without contributions from the district. Include a list of drawbacks for which you have already considered solutions. Explain how the project can tie into classroom-based assessments or curricula. Limit your sales pitch to five minutes and you will have cleared the way for many fruitful meetings in the future.

Next, woo the parents. Send home a combination info sheet and permission slip for any group of students with whom you will be working occasionally at nontraditional tasks. Limit it to one page, double-spaced, and make it large print and to the point. Be sure to include a nonparticipation option and specify alternative activities available to students (such as recreational reading or an online tutorial on information gathering). Include a line where parents can list any student limitations or allergies. Carefully file the permission slips. Where feasible, have the page translated into major languages spoken by your parents. Students are a possible source for very rough translations, but keep in mind that they probably have not been trained in writing a language spoken at home.

CHAPTER 12

Painting and Use of Color

 Inspiration. Interior design professionals often ask clients to choose an inspiration piece to help define color for a space. For a library, the inspiration is likely to come from a catalog of media center supplies. Flip through the pages until an item grabs your attention. Suppose a brightly colored bin-style book truck looks appealing. The design solves the problem of suicidal books jumping to the floor. On the same page is a rolling atlas/dictionary truck from the same company, so the styles are compatible. Both trucks came in a variety of colors and neutrals.

The safe choice, the prudent choice, is beige or black: on the other hand, vivid colors provide a distraction from existing 1970s chairs and pallid walls. This *could* compound the color problem. Instead, these two purchases create a powerful presence for modernity right at the library door and set the stage for purchases in years to come. Ask church/temple/club groups to purchase the first inspiration piece for a struggling library. Keep walls, shelving, tables, and blinds neutral so that future planners can add, subtract, or change accent colors with ease. Even these two colorful carts are reversible choices because an automotive paint shop can powder coat them in conservative colors.

 Use color chips wisely. Visit a paint department with catalog in hand. Find color chips that match current or projected furnishings. Clear plastic wallet inserts that normally hold photos are a great place to store paint chips, fabric samples or clippings cut from catalogs so that all the design elements are in one place.

 Choose a palette confidently. Paint departments are eager to help you make pleasing choices. Each paint company has brochures to show you combinations of colors chosen by professional designers. The calmest choice is to pick three colors from

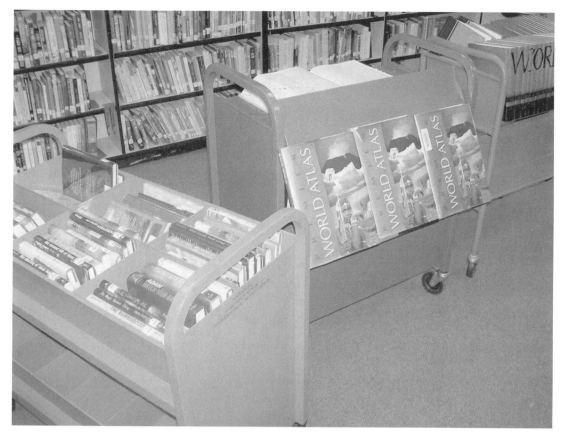

Figure 12.1 Inspiration carts

Figure 12.2 Wallet sampler

Figure 12.3 Paint chips

one paint chip, which produces a monochromatic palette. Consult a color wheel to explore complementary colors. The more adventuresome librarian can collaborate with the school art department. Another possible place to start is with *one* of the school colors.

Track down "Oops" paint. Stores have different names for the area where customers, dissatisfied with the color, return paint: "Oops," "Mis-mixed," "Clearance," or "Mark-downs." Having a color palette picked out makes it simple to solicit paint. Type the request on school letterhead. Letterhead is the first thing to feel the budget ax, so create letterhead of your own and keep it handy for this type of letter. (Your word processing program has templates for this.) Putting the request on letterhead makes for a professional interface. Carry the letter to the store, pick out miss-mixed paint from the "Oops area," and then ask the paint manager for the paint.

Interior paints only. Presenting a busy manager with the letter and its modest fulfillment all at one time often yields quick results. It is likely that you will come back to the library with more paint than initially requested. It may take more than one store to find mistake paints that are close to your palette. Since they are free, be flexible. Ideally you would choose low VOC (volatile organic compounds) paints, but these do not end up in the Oops area. Do pick interior paints only. Choose at least one can of white latex to tone down colors that are too bright or dark. Experiment back at the school.

Figure 12.4 "Oops" paint cans

 Ask for a few painters' caps at the same time. Kids and teens love painters' caps for different reasons. Paint sticks are usually free, but limit the number. They make excellent handles for signs and shadow puppets as well as paint stirrers.

 Keep paint off the students and parents off your back. After student painters give you their signed (not forged) permission slips, have them remove their shoes and socks. Parents pay a ransom for shoes, so getting paint on them is a major gaffe. Second, bare feet *feel* spilled paint better than shod feet, so people track less paint on library floors. Have students remove hooded sweatshirts and roll up jeans and shirtsleeves.

 Get 50-gallon plastic trash bags from the custodian. Cut out slits for the arms and head. Save these heavy-duty bags for future repeat use. Smaller children will fit into waste basket-size bags. Tie back long hair with a disposable elastic band or provide disposable shower caps. Stockpile free, packaged motel shower caps from staff vacations.

 Value real wood. If the library has real wood in good condition do not paint over it. Walls are for painting: wood is not. If the wood looks seriously dated, see if maintenance staff can lighten, darken, or freshen it. Stripping is too much work, but a good scrubbing or pickling (with diluted white paint) may be worthwhile. It is also easy to darken lackluster surfaces or trim moldings with Old English Furniture Polish. Care-

Figure 12.5 Garbage sacks

fully discard polish rags because they are flammable. Do this type of project when students are absent.

If the wood look is actually laminate or paper-printed paneling, then paint is a great solution. Primer may be necessary. Marked down primer is often in the "Oops" area as well, so keep an eye out for it. Shiny, slick, or glossy surfaces may need a light sanding before priming. Students may sand laminate, but *never* have them sand old paint (which may contain lead). Paint old laminate furniture the same color as the wall to minimize and modernize it. The used, magazine-shelving unit (Figure 12.6) was formerly fake walnut. With fresh paint and updated safety hinges, it is good for many more years of service.

Visually this unit fades back to blend with the background wall. Use scraps of bright-colored laminate or paint from other library projects to tie orphan pieces of furniture into the whole scheme.

Inspect student work immediately. Whenever students paint, they invariably use too much paint even after instruction. The librarian will need to put in about five minutes of work to brush out drips and probably another few minutes to finish the student cleanup of brushes. Snag cheap or free plastic plates, cups, or cartons at garage sales or use yogurt cups from the teachers lounge as throwaway paint containers that need no scrubbing. Disposable, one-inch foam brushes (frequently on sale for 10 cents each) conserve time and water.

Paint pads. Paint pads with plastic handles are easier to use than rollers, absorb less paint, and clean up with less water so they are a sound ecological choice.

Tape removes drips. One way to remove a still damp drip in an otherwise well-painted area is to wrap a piece of masking tape around three fingers (sticky side out) and gently tap the tape over the drip. The tape will remove excess paint.

Bright laminate. Formica or Wilson Art laminates solve many design dilemmas. Laminate is inexpensive and easy to apply on straight, flat surfaces such as

Figure 12.6 Magazine storage

a damaged counter. Discuss your proposed plan with your supervisor, getting the okay in writing or e-mail. The local public library or home improvement store will have instruction books to borrow or photocopy. Internet how-tos may also suffice. Here are two hints they may leave out: draw the cutting line on masking tape instead of directly on the laminate. Sawing through the tape will reduce the possibility for ragged edges or splits. Also, lay several dowels between the two surfaces to be adhered with contact cement to enable easy placement without premature adhesion.

Shop class. Enlist a high school shop teacher to have a class do the laminate cuts if you are not handy with a band saw. Then even younger library patrons can propose a pattern for the laminate pieces. Preschoolers and kindergartners dry lay the pieces in a design (similar to a quilt), which an adult will adhere in their absence. Middle school and senior high school students can take more responsibility for the end product. Use environmentally friendly contact cement. Patron involvement and subsequent pride is essential to the success of a Shoestring Library.

Win over maintenance people. Maintenance staffers are probably facing the same budget constraints as the library and a similar workload: commiserate with them. A treat such as ice cream bars (sale-priced, of course) on a hot summer day when they are at work (and you are not!) can build a relationship of mutual appreciation. Acknowledging the difficulties under which they work will go a long way toward putting library projects on the short list.

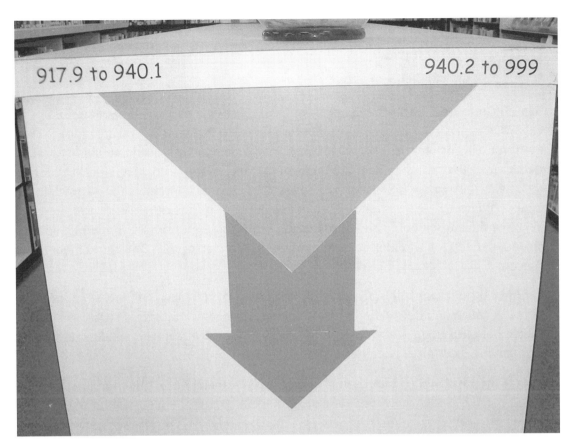

Figure 12.7 Endcaps in laminate

Maintain boundaries. As a professional, work sensibly with union custodians, painters, and repair people. Most librarians do not earn a degree in order to run a vacuum. Librarians want to work with patrons and media. In your enthusiasm to create great spaces, it is possible to go overboard on the cleaning and sprucing. Quiz staff about what it is appropriate to tackle yourself. Decorative painting is fine for library staff and students: whole rooms done with rollers generally are not. For safety, use extension poles rather than ladders when possible. Leave projects that make huge permanent library changes to administrators or maintenance people. Keep *your* projects reversible.

Accent wall. With the warning about not stepping on the toes of union painters, it is still possible to paint one accent wall to give a wallop of color for a minimum of time and money expended. Avoid red, black, and purple or any super-saturated colors as these take as many as five coats to cover completely and two coats of primer to remove when they are no longer wanted.

Paint plastic. Purchase at least one can of fusion-style spray paint to match the color scheme. This paint bonds with plastic at the molecular level so that it will not peel off. Give bland office supplies such as staplers, phones, wire baskets, or even a wastebasket a punch of color. Apply spray paint with a very light dusting of color to avoid drips. When possible, spray horizontal surfaces as opposed to vertical. For example, tip an old desk onto its back to paint the front. Each coat dries to the touch in 12 minutes, so four light coats are possible in one hour. Some of these hints about changing library furnishings are feasible because you are the one who has obtained the used furniture in the first place. If the item belongs to the district, get permission. Where feasible, paint outside.

 Match containers and office supplies. A color scheme narrows the search for accessories: objects in the sought-after color attract your notice. If you are on the lookout for a school color, it is surprising how many inexpensive, used containers exist in the target hue. All the matching items in the following photo cost under one dollar total at various garage sales and free boxes. Use colored containers for pushpins, treats, safe liquid cleaners carefully labeled, paper clips and other office supplies. Whether the chosen color is neutral, pastel, or bright, the uniformity creates a cohesive look. Each jolt of color costs about a dime and carries the color throughout the space.

Colored binders and files. Colored binders, plastic envelopes, and portable file bins can create an effect called color blocking. Instead of painting an area, a dozen shelved binders in the same color will read as a solid. Collect used binders, rather than buying them all at once new.

Touch-up paint. When purchasing *vividly colored* metal book trucks, chairs, or display stands, order matching aerosol spray paint from the manufacturer at the

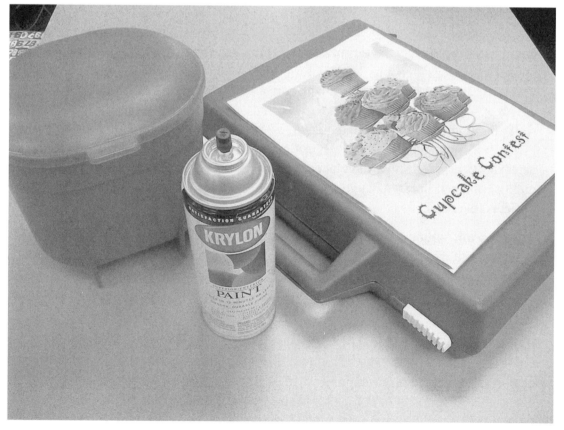

Figure 12.8 Painting plastic

Figure 12.9   Plastic items

Figure 12.10   Color blocking with binders

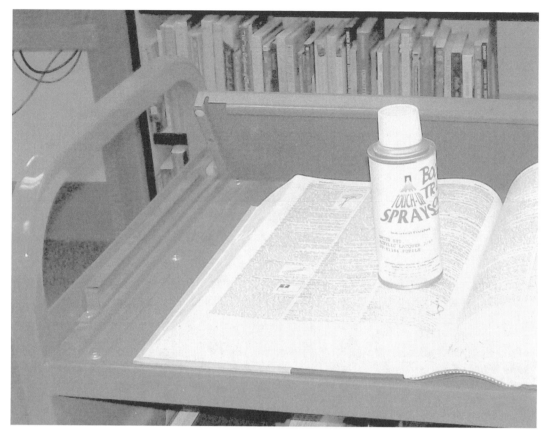

Figure 12.11   Touch-up paint

same time for the inevitable touch ups as nicks and dings occur. This protects your investment and keeps the library looking shipshape.

Always order matching spray paint from the manufacturer for colored metal furnishings.

 Disposal of "Oops" paint. Paint cans do not go in the regular trash. Set them out for the building custodian. Paint is combustible, so discard promptly. Throw away any used rags immediately.

Paint a card. During cleanup, paint a standard 3 × 5 card. When it is dry, describe the paint project on the back. This will simplify computerized color-matching service in the future if you ever have to buy more paint. It also helps you look for "Oops" paint in a similar colorway.

Never paint from the can. Never, ever let kids paint directly from the cans. Pour paint into nontip containers. Also, choose water wash-up *latex* paints. Do not use oil-base paints. Have plenty of dry rags, wet rags, and paper towels at hand. Ask parents via newsletter for the donation of clean shop towels, rags, or old tee shirts. Cotton swabs (requested from the school nurse) are also helpful. When it is necessary to use a roller tray, spread newspapers on a table to keep the tray off the floor and spread a heavy-duty plastic tarp under the table.

 Inexpensive canvas drop cloths are often too porous to keep paint off rugs. When possible move the item to be painted off the carpet. It is much easier to clean paint off hard surfaces than from soft ones.

Picture a teen in size 12 Nikes stepping into a paint tray and then racing the length of the carpet to wash off his precious shoe.

 Gadgets. Each year sees new paint gadgets and masking products that are great alternatives for children and teens. Some allow painting without the use of ladders or trays. They reduce spills and waste. Visit a paint department to see what is currently cutting-edge.

CHAPTER 13

Ceilings

Limit ladders. To limit the use of ladders, have maintenance personnel install a few permanent chains from high ceilings or stretch airplane wire across a library between eyehooks for suspending displays. Borrow or purchase a four-foot-wide, folding work platform that is only 18 inches from the floor, for supervised older students. These are available at home improvement stores for less than $25 and include a shelf for paint supplies and towels.

Magnetic hooks. Simple magnetic hooks are inexpensive and available at many hardware stores, but they are not strong enough to support heavy items. They are a great way to hang strings of holiday lights such as red peppers or summer dragonflies. Such lights usually go on sale half-price the day after a holiday and 75% off several days later, but if lights are in short supply they may sell out at full price. If a particular color or style is essential, consider paying list price. Use magnet hooks to support streamers, posters, or garlands from steel door or window casings. Magnets are far more reliable than masking tape.

Use an extend-a-reach grabber to lift items overhead. Some brands last longer than others. The types with square, ridged grippers are more durable than the ones with round, rubber tips attached to springs.

Barnacle clips. Barnacle clips are metal clips that attach to a grid ceiling to provide secure hooks for items weighing several pounds. With a little effort they can be moved anywhere the grid extends. These are commonly available at hardware stores or by catalog.

Figure 13.1   Magnet hooks

Figure 13.2   Barnacle clips. Kimono

Magnetic grid clips. Square magnetic ceiling grid clips have very powerful magnets, which hold up to 10 pounds and are much easier to install than barnacle clips. Order these more expensive clips from catalogs or online. They are much stronger than the round magnet hooks commonly sold in hardware stores.

Heavy-duty monofilament clear fishing line. Clear fishing line comes in many weights, from the thin line intended for fish under 8 pounds on up to thicker line for 20-pound monsters of the deep. Keep in mind that even though the line may support 20 pounds, the ceiling grid may not. Because the line is clear, display items appear to float without distracting strings or chains showing. New monofilament line is not cheap: find partial reels at estate sales.

Large paper clips. In a pinch, use large paper clips to display lightweight paper items from a grid ceiling. Use one loop as the hook and straighten the other loop to slide between the grid and the tile, being careful not to nick or scar the acoustic tile.

Umbrellas and parasols. Use open umbrellas suspended from the ceiling by their handles as bright seasonal decorations. Chinese paper umbrellas are particularly beautiful when lit from above by the library fluorescent lights. Use standard umbrellas to collect new socks for homeless people: patrons throw donations overhead. Red or pink umbrellas can collect aerial paper valentines. The umbrellas do not have to have a purpose: beauty, fun, and whimsy are ends in themselves.

Figure 13.3 Umbrellas

Canes, crutches, artificial limbs, and related media. Many teen novels deal with the loss of mobility often related to drunk driving or disease. Younger children have storybooks about broken bones. Ask the school nurse to lend crutches to suspend from the ceiling. Couple the display with books sharing this theme.

Oddly enough, it is possible to purchase prostheses at garage sales or borrow them from veterans' associations. An artificial leg in a cowboy boot or sequined cross trainer can stir up lively discussion. Use this ceiling treatment if the community has an alcohol or drug abuse emphasis such as Red Ribbon Week. It is appropriate for Veterans Day combined with military uniforms. Use for social studies units on land-mines or IEDs (improvised explosive devices).

Kites. Nylon rip stop kites can provide a burst of ceiling color. Display several kites at once or rotate through a collection of kites. Kites collect dust easily so clean them every few months.

Flags are ideal overhead teaching aids. Request the loan of historic flags or flags from the travels of other teachers. Follow flag etiquette, keeping flags off the floor and with the band or grommet edge nearest the ceiling. For very large flags, attach all four corners to the ceiling with the center billowing downward so there is room to walk underneath it.

Figure 13.4 Prosthesis

Figure 13.5 Ship kite

Figure 13.6 Flags

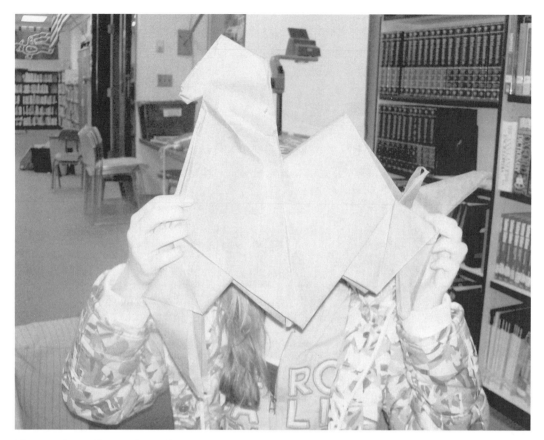

Figure 13.7   Giant origami horse

 Giant origami. Use a piece of butcher paper that is as long as it is wide, often one yard square. Enlist a student to fold it into a giant origami such as red lips with taped-on white fangs for Halloween or an immense white crane to support mental health. Many students know how to fold an origami box (the kind that inflates with a puff of air). Draft them to make some large versions from old National Geographic maps. Suspend with clear fishing line.

Ceiling damage. Flat-roofed libraries may suffer from continued leaks during hard economic times. After the leaks are fixed, the resulting stains blight library appearance. Use an aerosol spray specifically designed to hide damage to ceiling tiles without having to remove the tiles. It has a nozzle that successfully sprays upward.

Do not forget other ideas for suspended ceiling décor in chapter 9.

CHAPTER 14

Increase Seating

 Narrow window counters. Take advantage of any narrow spaces between windows and book stacks. While they may be too narrow for traditional library tables, they can be perfect for bar-height counters. Kids love the views. Ask maintenance staff to install a simple 18-inch-deep counter supported by 2 × 4 knee braces strengthened with plywood triangles. Cut a sheet of 3/4-inch plywood into several 18″ × 72″ panels for the counters. Cover the plywood with neutral or colored laminate. Laminates now mimic a stunning array of natural materials and textures. Edge the counter with a 1 × 2 faced with a matching strip of laminate.

 Secondhand barstools. Used barstools are common, but sometimes rickety. Tighten all screws or joints. Ask maintenance department for an appropriate glue, but keep in mind that no amount of gluing is equal to the rigors of one tipping patron. Before purchasing a used stool, put it to a vigorous test and reject it if any safety issue appears. Sears Craftsman stools can work well for libraries, but the best stool is all one piece with no movable parts and no upholstery.

 Dedicated stools. If your area has churches, temples, mosques, or synagogues, contact them with a request to purchase one or more new stools in honor of their students. If you can name students from their congregation, your request has more power. That is not as difficult as it seems. Students talk about their youth group activities. Ask them who attends. Make lists or ask the kids to make the lists. Public libraries can solicit from fraternal groups, veterans' organizations, and auxiliaries. College libraries can solicit from Greek societies, alumni groups, and other campus

Figure 14.1   Knee brace counter

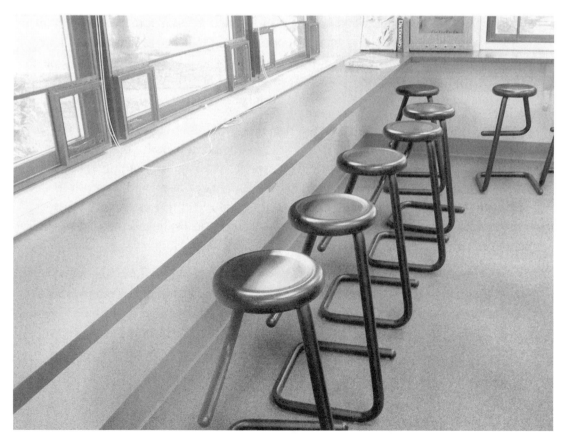

Figure 14.2   Donor stools

organizations. Once stools are donated, print up the name of the donor organization and attach it to the stool leg with clear library tape.

 Prototype. When dealing with administrators, a donated prototype or sample shows possibilities. Sometimes a librarian has to communicate a vision of what the library can be by giving tangible examples. Then the district can flesh out the vision. Considerable pride will attach to those first donated stools, satisfaction that can lead to district purchases.

 Banks, dentists, doctors and other public offices. Local professional offices occasionally upgrade their furniture. If community members identify the librarian as someone always on the lookout for recycled items, they may contact the library to donate their old chairs, file cabinets, and tables. To be proactive, drop a professionally worded e-mail or letter to businesses asking that they keep you in mind for possible future donations. Accept as much as possible, sharing any surplus with other classrooms, schools, or organizations.

 Pragmatic publicity. Follow up with thank you notes and with publicity *if the business wants it.* A brief e-mail to the community news desk of a local newspaper serves two purposes: good press for the business and a consumer alert as to the willingness of the library to accept donations of goods. Local libraries benefit from upholstered chairs, tables, file cabinets, desk chairs, office mats, a kick stool, and even movable steps.

Figure 14.3 Chairs from bank

Thrift store furniture. Depending on the size of the community, thrift stores offer great bargain opportunities. Stores related to a charity such as The Salvation Army, Goodwill, Value Village, Y's Buys (YWCA), and Saint Vincent DePaul are more frequently the recipients of business cast-offs, which often include matched sets of padded chairs with reasonably modern wooden arms and frames. In addition, your library dollars will go to support worthwhile community programs such as worker training and sheltered workshops.

 No purchases orders. One difficulty in purchasing from thrift stores is that they may not accept school purchase orders. This may be a good place to use the one percent you designated from your salary, especially if the purchase would increase both functionality and beauty. Plus, good quality matching furniture would probably disappear before a purchase order could be issued.

 Rubber cement thinner removes sticky price tag residue from used furniture. Before spending money, ask the custodian for an industrial-strength wood cleaner for use when students are absent from the building. (The thinner also works on glue residue from barcodes or spine labels on books. Even if you do not use rubber cement, keep the thinner on hand.)

 Microfiber cloths. Ask an adult volunteer to clean one chair with a microfiber cloth and a spray-on upholstery cleaner that has either enzymes or oxygen bleach. Custodial staff at a Shoestring Library are hard-pressed to shampoo *rugs* once per year without taking on upholstery.

Figure 14.4 Thrift store chairs, table

Kids clean low. Child volunteers can clean with warm water in a spray bottle and a microfiber cloth. These cloths are more hygienic than sponges and more efficient at removing soil. Since children are closer to the ground, get them to clean legs or end panels of tables.

 Vacuum upholstered furniture annually. Put in a written request asking custodial staff to vacuum any upholstered furniture at least once per year. If they cannot allot time for that, borrow their backpack or handheld vacuum for a volunteer or older patron to use.

 Wash furniture the Shoestring way. If a responsible adult is available, move plastic furniture or metal carts into a shower or pressure wash area, often located near the gym or bus garages. Car washing brushes and rubbing compound can give new life to old metal furnishings as well. If experimenting with items where overspray may hit fabric, clean right before a weekend, so furniture will have a chance to dry.

 Commercial carwashes. Hand-held carwash wands are great for doing a batch of chairs at once. Pile nonupholstered furnishings into a pickup or open trailer to transport.

They may not even need to be unloaded to wash. This is one time you do not want to recycle; some carwashes reuse their gray water repeatedly except for the rinse cycle. Avoid this by using the spray wands, which generally use clean water. For most chairs, the high pressure spray wand works better than the brush wand.

Figure 14.5 Carwashed furniture

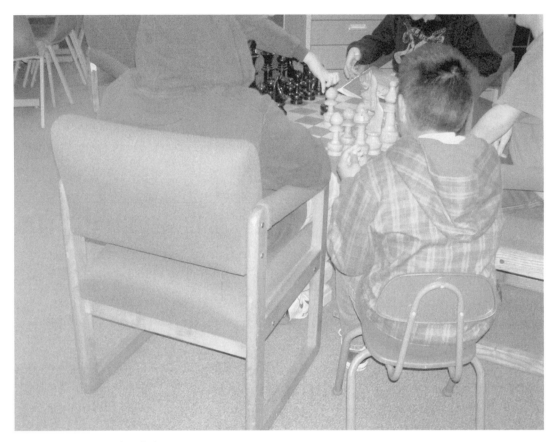

Figure 14.6   Preschool chairs

 Tiny chairs solve big problems. Baby chairs are endearing. The short, sturdy little chairs of childhood have many benefits in libraries designed for older patrons. Brightly colored, stackable, and washable preschool chairs are extremely portable and store in limited space. A scattering of mini-chairs allows patrons to huddle. Two or three people can work in close proximity on a project in the space of one office-size chair. Verify the maximum load to ascertain if the chair is strong enough to support an average adult. Select chairs designed for school use, not chairs with plastic legs available for home use.

CHAPTER 15

Shelving and Desk Solutions

Repurposed commercial shelving. Joanne's is a nationwide chain of fabric and craft stores. They have a generous discount card available for teachers and librarians, but more than that, they frequently rearrange their stores. They are a possible source for free dowels, free heavy cardboard tubes, and, rarely, free Plexiglas shelves designed to hold craft magazines. Use the Plexiglas on top of standard shelving to display quick reads or picture books. The tabs, visible in the following picture, could be removed with a hacksaw, but these shelves are used *as is* to save time. In addition, this store frequently marks down seasonal items 75% as well as offering newspaper or subscriber coupons. You may find free items by their curb. Also check with Michael's and other national, regional, or local craft stores.

Neon-colored clear vinyl. Fabric and craft stores such as Joanne's and Michael's are a source for colored vinyl by the yard in *clear* teal, purple, pink, and other vibrant colors that make great covers to enliven computer tables for less than $2 per table. Disguise old or dinged up desks with covers that are easy to wipe clean. The brightly colored, clear vinyl conveys a fresh modern look without looking like a tablecloth. Expand this popular see-through neon color to other secondhand accessories made of clear vinyl, acrylic, and Plexiglas such as lamps, tissue dispensers, and frames.

Serendipitous finds. On the window ledge behind the printer in Figure 15.2 are free, jazzy glass panels from pinball machines, which promote the librarian's favorite authors. This is a case of finding something odd and turning it into a library tool. No one shops for pinball machine panels at a rummage sale, but librarians

Figure 15.1 Plexiglas shelving

Figure 15.2 Vinyl table covers

should be alert to serendipitous finds. When you see something unique and cheap, brainstorm ways you could adapt it to serve in your library.

 Forage far afield. The sturdy metal stool in the foreground of the previous photo is one of three from the district's aged surplus, which students painted with "Oops" paint. Do not limit your searches to your own campus: request permission to explore other schools and libraries in the district for their surplus as well.

 Lurking in alleys. Retail stores and offices often leave items for trash disposal in their alleys. Librarians have found usable file cabinets and spinner display units to adapt for library use. These are not *forever* finds, but they tide a library over until the budget improves. It is courteous to check with the business before hauling them off.

 Refreshing old shelves. Shelves do not seem to have a shelf life. They just go on holding things up stolidly for years, but eventually they may sag. Make it a point to clear off one shelf periodically and flip it over if possible to reverse the sag. Not all shelves lend themselves to this treatment, but you can prolong the life of many medium density fiberboard (MFD) shelves by flipping.

(This is an excellent large muscle activity for students who need to calm themselves.)

This is also a good time to weed that shelf, pull damaged items, and add reading levels. Weeding tends to be a nonpriority until the library runs out of space. Tackle one shelf occasionally to break this chore into manageable chunks.

 Bookstops. Librarians obsess about edging the collection (bringing all books up to the edge of the shelves to make them easier to find and to look tidy). If you have paperbacks or novels stored in deep shelves, make bookstops from free wood. The bookstop prevents the book from sliding to the back of the bookshelf. A bookstop should be the length of the shelf, about 3/4-inch high and wide enough to fit snugly *behind* the books. Obsolete, discarded bookshelves are good to cut up lengthways for this purpose and yield two bookstops each, roughly 36 × 5 × 3/4 inches.

Add casters to old shelf units. Libraries serve many community functions, and flexibility is essential. Empty an old, low shelving unit and turn it upside down for the simple installation of six heavy-duty casters. These are about eight inches tall. Position them in as wide a stance as possible to keep the shelving from tipping. Casters differ from wheels in that they can swivel. Now the mobile shelves can meander to any part of the library.

If you rearrange the library often to accommodate book fairs, faculty meetings, or public functions, this type of mobile shelving can simplify the process. It also allows the shelves to condense into a smaller area to accommodate large group seating for board meetings or programs. Loaded, this unit will be so heavy that locking wheels are not essential.

 Double-sided book trucks instead of stationary shelves. These five-foot-tall, double-sided book trucks allow huge numbers of books to be moved any place in the library that needs a feature collection. Two of these trucks house a tribal history

Figure 15.3 Attach casters

collection, Native American fiction, and a fantasy collection. Later, the side filled with history primary resources will be rotated into the main aisle. Move them into more prominent positions in response to curriculum emphases. Book trucks are usually much shorter and used only for library jobs, but these 60-inch versions with locking wheels are a superior alternative for flexible permanent storage and display of hundreds of volumes. Propose these for grant funds.

 Recycling furniture with a sledge hammer. Schools occasionally discard ancient *oak* cabinets, shelves, or desks too battered to sell as surplus. Sledgehammer these into manageable-size boards to use in simple projects.

 No-cost computer stand. Figure 15.5 showcases one such project: a free computer stand. A simple shelf attached to the wall and standing on two legs makes a free piece of furniture to serve the specific need for a stand-up, dash-and-browse catalog computer stand. This unit used one piece of plywood for the shelf (the size dictated by the scrap of space available and the size of the cumbersome old monitor). Nail three-inch-wide strips of oak together around the plywood with simple butt joints, no mitering necessary. Screw a wooden cleat into the wall to support the shelf. Make everything sturdy via two tall legs with a double crossbar. The four-foot-high legs create a comfortable standing height for teens and adults. Ask a handy

Figure 15.4   Tall movable shelves

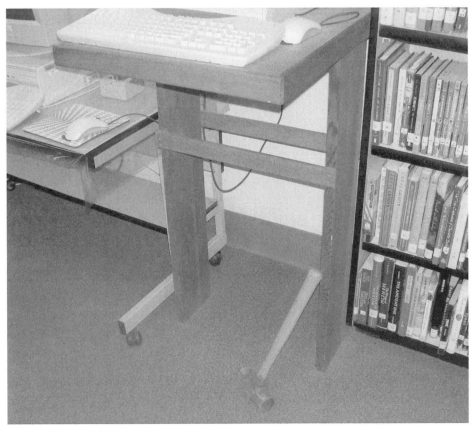

Figure 15.5   Computer stand and sledge hammer

parent or patron to do this type of project or request it from your maintenance staff. High schoolers can do it with supervision.

If possible, nail the cleat into studs, but in the absence of a suitable stud, use mollies. Simply drill a hole as per instructions on the container of plastic mollies, tap in the molly and then screw the cleat to the wall. If you have brick or plaster walls or metal studs, confer with building staff before considering a project like this.

 "I brake for free wood." Construction sites often have bins with signs for free wood scraps. So do home improvement stores. Since the average librarian is only tackling uncomplicated, one-hour projects with students or community helpers, scrap wood is often sufficient. Because these projects are not permanent additions, they are easily recycled during upgrades. Think of it as an intermittent material, temporarily useful in your library on its way to a bonfire or landfill.

 Update a painted desk. Steel grey office desks last forever, but enameled *drawers* date them with colors from the 1950s. Stripping an entire piece of furniture is too labor intensive, but emptying a few drawers, removing the hardware, and coating with an eco-friendly stripper takes less than an hour. A few drawers can be easily transported offsite, or maintenance staff can tackle this job in their shop area to protect students and staff from any fumes. Stripped drawers will eventually rust. Seal with a spray can of clear coat varnish. Strip only the drawer front. No one sees the interior or sides except the librarian. Alternatively, take a risk, and create some artsy, industrial swirls with a hand-held grinder or sander. Then seal.

Figure 15.6 Updating metal desk

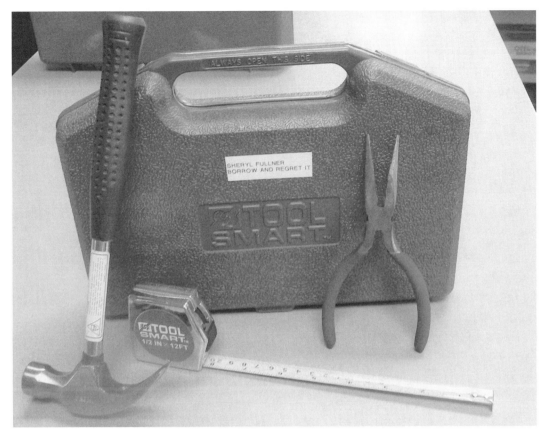

Figure 15.7 Tool kit empowerment

 Use beeswax as an alternative to sealer. Reapply annually

 Empowered by a tool kit. Holidays are good times to purchase compact, budget-priced tool kits. An ergonomic hammer, a tape measure, and Phillips and flat head screwdrivers are the most essential items. These are not so much for building or repairs (the maintenance staff does those), but they are handy for taking a photocopier drawer apart, hanging a piece of art, or measuring distances for library activities.

CHAPTER 16

Map the Library

Map the endcaps. Label the ends of stacks with call numbers typed on white paper and then burned onto a transparency with the photocopier. This allows unlimited fonts and sizes to fit the shelf edges exactly. Trim the numbers and then cover with clear, wide library tape. Where feasible, make the printing large enough to be visible from the reference desk. Using the transparency allows the color of the shelf to show through for a seamless appearance.

Map the cupboards and closets. Next, using the same method, number every cabinet in the library and in any storage or support rooms. This simplifies directing workers to the cabinets. Make a schematic to keep by the desk for quick reference. A faster method is simply to use a washable marker (such as a transparency marker) to number the cabinet doors and drawers. (Test a hidden surface for nonstaining washability first.) Label makers are also a possibility.

Repurpose paper ream boxes. Ask the office staff to save all *uniform,* heavy-duty paper ream boxes for the library. Nest each box in its lid to make it sturdier. Depending on the size of your cabinets, two or four boxes may fit easily. Label the front of each box boldly with a bright, large sticky note to indicate contents. Avoid permanent labels to facilitate quick changes.

For example, one cabinet might hold seasonal items, with boxes for spring, winter, summer, and fall. When it is time to use the contents, it is easy to slide out one box. Cabinets stay tidy and manageable. You can empty and search any cabinet in just a few motions. The beginning inventory is easy: for example, a simple label posted for cabinet four might say "Seasonal Decorations."

Figure 16.1 Mapping endcaps

Create a searchable inventory. Compiling the ongoing inventory is a good job for a library volunteer because it does not require the librarian's master computer. Make a list of the contents and their location, one cabinet at a time, then e-mail the data to the inventory folder. If the moose are missing, type "moose" into the search pane of the inventory folder or documents in general, and their location will pop up, cabinet six.

Divide this project into two parts. First, the list of what is actually in a cabinet can be handwritten on a clipboard. Second, the list can be transferred to computer or more simply done in one step with a laptop (which a Shoestring Library probably does not own).

Prefer clear plastic storage bins. If there is ever a budget for plastic storage bins, choose clear plastic to easily view and find contents. Opaque plastic increases the search time.

No-cost book maps. When there are limited funds for staff time to shelve books, the library is at the mercy of patrons' shelving attempts. The use of book dummies or proxies to direct patrons is common. Book dummies can be purchased from library supply catalogs. The book-shaped dummy is labeled with directions such as *Fiction HAP continues around the corner.* Instead of paying money for book dummies, solicit free old Reader's Digest Condensed books. Your local public library probably has an excess of these that have been donated for book sales.

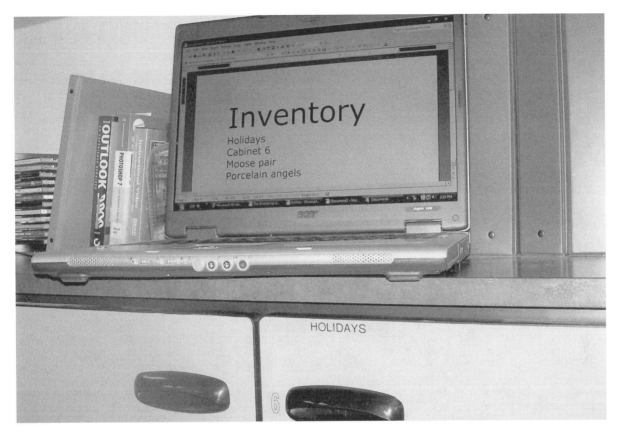

Figure 16.2 Inventory numbers on cabinets

Create a book dummy. Each bank of shelves in a Shoestring Library has a discarded Reader's Digest Condensed Book repurposed into a book dummy or book-map at the top and bottom of the stack with a typed label explicitly stating which call numbers belong in that section. The top left book map says: "The first book in this bank of shelves should be 363.6." The bottom right book map says: "The last book in this bank of shelves should be 387.9." Some of the book maps advise shelvers to look around the corner to avoid the dreaded *double run*.

(The Aurora public library describes a double run as the error when a duplicate set of call numbers or authors occurs at the end of one section and the beginning of another.) A book dummy or bookmap limits the chaos.

Tape on new numbers. Follow the acquisitions hints earlier in this book, and it may be necessary to relabel some book maps as shelves fill with new books. The yearly relabeling is tedious but only takes about an hour or two and keeps the books roughly where they belong. There is no need to be replace the whole label: merely tape on new numbers.

Avoid metal clips. Some libraries use horizontal metal clips to label the shelves; others use a label maker. Metal clips have gone out of favor as they may hamper shelving and tend to fall off. The adhesive labels for each shelf, specifying exactly what is on that shelf, are admirable, but need changing so often that they may be burdensome. For the relatively static library, they are a possibility. Avoid plastic signage that clips onto shelves (it has a high death rate).

Figure 16.3 Ream boxes for storage

 Magnetic shelf labels. If the shelves are metal, print information on commercially available magnetic shelf labels, which are easy to reposition or replace. Magnetic business cards are popular giveaways. Repurpose them into shelf labels. Cut them lengthwise into two long strips and face them with Dewey numbers attached with spray adhesive.

CHAPTER 17

Wise Lighting

Light meter the library. If it seems as though parts of the library are getting darker, use a light meter or your camera to measure and document the lumens. When districts decide to cut the budget stringently, lights are often the first thing to go. Make sure light reaches to the bottom shelves of nonfiction stacks. (Fiction is generally easier to locate in less than optimal conditions than are the challenging Dewey numbers for nonfiction. Library of Congress collections need generous lighting for all.)

Count the tubes. The circulation desk needs an extra fluorescent tube or two. Look up to examine the ceiling fixture above the desk and in student study areas. Maintenance workers often remove or replace tubes during vacations. For cost cutting, they are sometimes encouraged to limit fixtures to two tubes rather than four. Light-starved workers can request the return of a few tubes. Also, consider a natural or true-light lamp for your immediate work area.

Novelty lights. Garage sales are a great source for novelty lights: make sure they have an Underwriters Laboratory (UL) tag attached. Always test them before purchase. Lights are a useful mood booster, especially in northern climates and on dark winter days. As your stable of lights grows, swap one out every month for a fresh look.

Light timer. Put the novelty light on a four-hour timer to minimize the possibility of overheating and to reduce library power consumption. Make sure no flammable substances are nearby. Only run one novelty light at a time and be careful to turn it off when closing the library if a timer has not already been set to do so.

Figure 17.1 Novelty lights

 Compact fluorescents. Whenever possible replace incandescent light bulbs with compact fluorescents. These are especially valuable in light tables because they generate negligible heat.

 Electric candle. A single electric candle is useful to keep on hand for all types of memorials. Combine with a flag, flowers, a stuffed animal, or other evocative item to create a silent tribute for Veterans Day, Memorial Day, Holocaust Remembrance Day, or even a local tragedy such as a fatal car accident or a soldier killed in action. A battery-operated candle is easier to position in a hallway or near a doorway than a corded candle, but the cord version is reliable. (See hint for free batteries in chapter 6.)

Daisy chains. The fire department inspects many public buildings on a yearly basis. Examine the library for any daisy chain infractions. A daisy chain is when an outlet strip supports and supplies electricity to another outlet strip. Instead of an outlet with 5 items, suddenly there are 10 devices running off one outlet. This is a definite danger for overheating, fire, or product failure. One outlet strip with a surge protector is usually acceptable.

 Never drape cords over the edges of counters and desks. It is a simple matter to ask for permission to drill a hole for a cord in an unobtrusive spot. Students delight to use a brace and bit that is a little wider than the plug. Since this is a hand tool, it is suitable for any age.

Figure 17.2 Electric candle

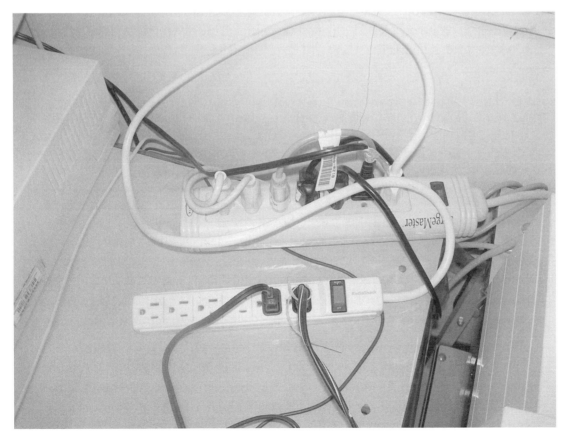

Figure 17.3 Daisy chain

Do not mistake a power strip for a surge protector. They look similar, but one functions only as a multi-outlet extension cord, while the other protects the plugged-in devices from electric surges common after power outages. Keep in mind that all extension cords are not created equal. Voltage may diminish when several cords are connected.

Clean windows. Clean windows flood an area with natural light. Put in a work request once per year to make sure this gets on the summer cleaning list. Natural light may reduce energy consumption. A Shoestring Librarian cannot assume that a Shoestring custodial staff will clean the whole library. Spell out your priorities.

Evaluate/eliminate drapes. Some libraries still have room-darkening drapes left over from the days of 16-millimeter and opaque projectors. These date a space and collect dust and allergens. If they are not used, take them down, fold them, and place them in large, labeled garbage bags in a back room or closet. If no one notices or complains after several months, consign them to the school building surplus area to be evaluated for possible sale by the administration. If that is approved, then ask the janitor to salvage the hardware as well.

Mini-blinds. Working horizontal slat shades may need to be adjusted seasonally or daily and occasionally dusted. It is usually cheaper and less frustrating to replace a mini-slat blind than to repair it (since it can take several hours to restring it). If it is broken and hanging crookedly, use monofilament line or lightweight string to tie it level with the header until it can be replaced. A crooked blind looks bad on the outside of the building as well as the inside.

Clean doors transmit light. If there is major glass in the library doors, make it your job to keep it relatively clean if the janitor cannot. That does not necessarily mean always washing it yourself.

Keep a jobs parking lot using sticky notes. Encourage teachers to send students who have finished their work to grab a chore off the parking lot when they come to the library for a book. Public and college libraries can keep job parking lots near the circulation desk or front door with a sign that says "Volunteer for Five Minutes!" A portable whiteboard helps match visitors with current quickie chores.

Be prepared with any supplies needed to tackle the listed jobs. If you have a job lot, keep a used plastic tote at hand with spray cleaner, glass cleaner, and paper towels. A scraper and staple remover are also possibilities. Here are three sample jobs: remove greasy forehead marks where patrons peer in, wash around the door handles, or remove scraps of tape left by posted notices. Clean glass doors contribute a great deal to a library's curb appeal. Even a once-a-month scrub will help.

Ceiling outlets. Ceiling outlets can provide a convenient and safe way to serve ceiling-mounted electronics and specialty lights. Request installation of a ceiling outlet rather than stringing extension cords. Map electrical needs and uses in the library. Do not passively accept the status quo without asking for improvements. District administrators may have a master plan for the ancient wiring, but it does not hurt to ask for minor updates ahead of a big future conversion.

Solar tubes. A Shoestring Librarian is often too busy to look at the big picture and may not be included on capital addition committees. Still, most committees welcome input. Submit a written request for upgraded lighting. As energy costs increase, ask them to consider the possibility of adding roof-mounted solar tubes to illuminate narrow areas such as library restrooms or stacks that are far from windows. A solar tube uses a mirrored, reflective surface to multiply the amount of natural light reaching the library. Even if the roof is not immediately above the library, sometimes the solar tube can slant light through attic or other space.

Compared to other renovations, solar tubes are a good value. In addition, they may provide some daylight when storms cause power outages. Do not feel badly if your proposal does not make the cut. Prolific idea people cannot afford to have ego connected to their many suggestions.

CHAPTER 18

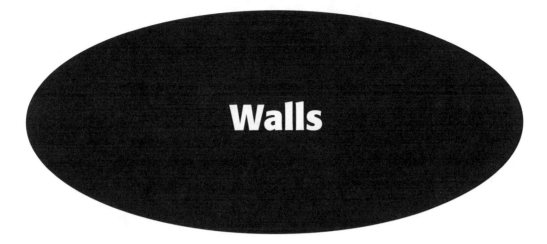

Walls

 Written or initialed administrative approval. Each wall project needs administrative approval as outlined in the introduction to section 2 of this book.

 Magical Masonite. Masonite comes in 4 × 8–foot sheets and is inexpensive. Many famous artists use this in preference to canvas because of its multiple virtues. It does not need stretching on wood frames. There is no stapling. The surface is smooth and accepts paint well. For librarians, there are even more benefits.

 First is the safety factor. Lean Masonite against a wall where even the youngest students can reach it without using ladders. Second, it fills a huge amount of space for a minuscule amount of money. It is very light to hang safely with a few screws. Trim it to fit irregular spaces. If students (or you) are not entirely satisfied with the final product, it is easy to amend with more paint.

 Plexiglas protection. If a mural is painted directly on the library wall (popular in many schools) cover it with a sheet of Plexiglas to protect from vandalism or wear. Often students will approach a mural innocently and touch the portion they painted, eventually wearing down the paint. These little bald spots multiply. Plexiglas is expensive, but usually only one mural per year is completed. Your initial project plan should include the Plexiglas cost.

Motto or logo. If a motto or school logo is part of the library décor, have students choose a font and make a transparency with several different sizes on one page. Then use an overhead projector to determine the size that best fits the space. Have the students outline the design with a washable black transparency marker. When the design is satisfactory, have them go over the ink with a permanent marker. Then,

Figure 18.1 Masonite Pioneer 10 spacecraft

Figure 18.2 Covered wagon heads for the stars

use a damp sponge over the whole design to remove the original washable marker. The washable marker lets you or your volunteers remove or repair any mistakes before inking in the final product. Use acrylic paints to fill in color. Acrylics are very user friendly and do not have any noxious fumes. They are also less likely to stain clothing.

Three-dimensional wall art. Anything involving a saw is a popular enrichment project. Make sure you have a parent consent form on file. Librarians do not always have their own classes, but there is no lack of students in the library. Librarians often cover entire classes so the teachers can have prep periods. In addition, librarians should be teaching groups of students information literacy. While the district may dictate the curriculum, the methods can be flexible. The following 3-D wall mural matches mandated content. These library art projects constitute a *tiny fraction* of students' library time and serve as both incentive and reward for the more challenging academic activities.

Begin with research. First, each student researches a favorite undersea creature to sketch, paint, cut out, and glue to a block of wood that the custodian will fasten to the finished wall. Then, using a long extension pole with a roller attached, students paint the boiler room or basement wall graduated shades of blue after discussing whether water is lighter or darker near the surface. At that point, students cut designs out of sponges or Styrofoam meat trays to create their own stamps. They use acrylic paint to stamp seaweed patterns to give the mural depth as high as they can safely reach.

Plywood or foamcore. Build this particular mural with donated 3/8-inch used plywood or use scissors to make equally handsome 3-D walls with cardstock or

Figure 18.3 Pioneers Lead

Figure 18.4   A 3-D fish memorial in boiler room

foamcore. If using plywood, safety is the first consideration. Some parents are eager for older students to have challenges such as working with a low-powered jigsaw or wood-burning tool under extremely vigilant supervision (for example, the student places both hands on the saw and the librarian keeps her hand between the student and the lightweight blade). Sixth graders can manage the project from early sketches through research stage to final artistic completion. Each step of the project is tied to a classroom-based assessment (CBA) that couples brain work with handiwork to everyone's satisfaction. Alternatively, have a parent helper do the sawing, allotting the researching, drawing, and painting to students.

Corrugated metal. For an industrial look for your library, consider two corrugated metal roofing panels (2 × 8 feet) on an accent wall. The metal can be new or used. Contact your local recycled building materials store for the best price. Choose other metal or stainless steel accessories to carry through on this theme. Corrugated metal is quick to install and remove. Attach a piece of wood lath along the bottom of the wall and another at the 7.5-foot mark. Then secure the panels to the lath to minimize the number of holes in the wall.

CHAPTER 19

Glass, a Clear Winner

DIY. (Do it yourself.) Some children served by a Shoestring Library live in desperate poverty: homes without running water or heat. It seems important to inform their sense of beauty along with their love of reading. The tiny amounts spent on these glass projects (from kitsch to fine art) are not enough to alleviate their poverty but can enlighten their spirits. The last three ideas seem ambitious during a depressed economy, but community support makes them feasible. Some states and provinces mandate one-half of one percent of a public building's cost be dedicated to art. Schools may content themselves with a concrete sign to meet that requirement, but often there is local backing to be a little more creative with an existing building. Talk to artists, quiz craftspeople, and court civic groups that might help you improve both your school and your library. Of course there is always that superb North American mantra, if all else fails, DIY, do it yourself.

Temporary glass paints. Glass paints are a quick, fun, cheap way for the nonartistic person to dress up a glass entrance door. Choose a simple design to pounce on the glass with applicators that are no more complex than liquid shoe polish. Students clean up by removing the paint with paper towels or a scraper.

Holiday window clings. Vinyl window clings are a foolproof and speedy way to create a festive entrance. Clings usually cost $1 or $2 for an 11 × 17 sheet with multiple designs but often go on sale for a quarter of that. Stockpile clings for all the seasons. Clings do not work well on doors or windows that experience extremes of cold or heat. No glue is involved, just static cling. Interior glass works best. Wash the glass thoroughly before adhering the cling to avoid transfer of dirt. Combine several sheets of clings to create a large border on a door's glass instead of sprinkling them

Figure 19.1   Scatter kindness

sparsely over the surface. Massing hearts, leaves, or snowpeople provides a far more powerful visual. Keep an eye out for clings in foreign languages that support a library's cross-cultural outreach.

 Cleaning clings. Do not hesitate to tie elements together by uncapping a fistful of *washable,* overhead projector markers and holding three or four in one hand make swirls to unite the clings. Experiment with decorating both sides of the glass for depth. Clings do lose their clinginess eventually, but renew them by a quick swish in hot, sudsy water. Decorating with clings is a great job for students: avoid the temptation to micromanage their production.

 Glass vases as sculpture. Perhaps because famous glass artist Dale Chihuly is a native of our state, vivid glassworks appeal as a strong way to add beauty and drama to a library. Purchase a few mass-produced *giant* glass vases (up to two feet tall). Watch for clearance vases from stores such as T.J. Maxx or Ross for Less for under $15 per vase. The cost is less than a bevy of library posters and makes a powerful design statement that can grow and develop over the years. Students have their tastes informed in a way that cartoon posters can not equal. Plus, even the rowdiest patrons are careful to protect the glass.

 Backlight with rope lights. When displaying any type of glass, try to backlight it with a rope light laid on the rear of the shelf.

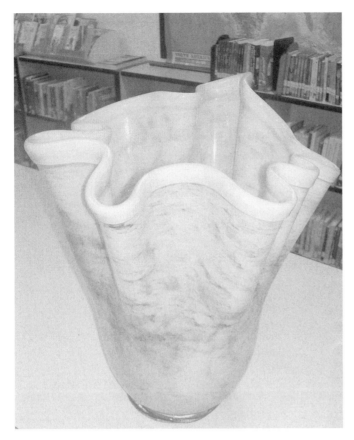

Figure 19.2   Inspiring vase

 Aquarium as exhibit case. While a large glass exhibit case is not a priority purchase for a Shoestring Library, there are times when it would be useful to show students precious, but untouchable, artifacts related to curriculum or featured titles. Free, leaky aquariums are common finds at garage sales and in the giveaway column in local online classifieds. Scrub the aquarium and turn it upside down over any display. The weight of the piece keeps it in place and it loses its fishy identity when flipped upside down. For a more permanent display, place peel and stick letters on the glass to describe the contents or donor.

 Glass block can be functional, dated, ugly, or artsy. Rearrange a circulation desk or counter to include glass blocks lit from behind with colored LED (light emitting diode) holiday lights. LEDs take very little electricity and do not overheat. Glass block also comes in many colors, patterns, and sizes. The used block pictured in the following image was discovered in an alley, and the owner agreed to donate it all to the library for use in the circulation desk. If the blocks are not stacked, it is safe to use them without mortar. Here, wood molding encloses the blocks. Acrylic blocks are also available.

 Reversible glass projects. Add removable beauty to the library by installing the glass project over existing windows using simple metal strips and uninstall it with a screwdriver.

Figure 19.3 Inverted aquarium display case

Figure 19.4 Glass block backlit with colored lights

The simplest and least expensive project is glass etching. Check with the local glass dealer to see if used plate glass is available. Have it cut to size and have the sharp edges removed. (This edge buffing costs money but is worth it for ease of handling panels.) Choose a silhouette, border or lettering. Cover the whole piece of glass, front and back, with a resist such as Contact paper or the heavier sand blasting paper available from funeral monument dealers. Cut out the design and remove the resist.

The reason for placing the Contact paper on the back is that when washing off the acid, it is easy to transfer some of it to the unprotected back glass and mar it.

Using rubber gloves, apply etching medium according to the directions on the jar. Remember that you are trying for a uniformly even surface. Bristle or lap marks will show up as lines. Etching medium is cheap and often available at craft stores for 40 percent off when using a coupon.

Sandblasting glass. A double thickness of adhesive paper is used if you are sand blasting instead of acid etching. Sand blasting gives a deeper design. For crafty people, sand blasting is fun to try; it *does* sting. Alternatively have it done by an auto body (not automotive) repair shop, preferably one owned by a friend of the library. Also find sand blasting in the yellow pages.

Stained glass. Stained glass is a pricey project, perhaps more suitable for a public or university library. Two ways to reduce the cost are to handle the design in-house. Find an attractive, copyright-free line drawing that would lend itself to simple glass cuts. An antique coloring book or beloved children's book may offer some ideas. Photocopy the line drawing onto a transparency. Using an overhead projector, transfer the design onto the window lined with butcher paper. Fit the design to the

Figure 19.5 Sandblasted silhouette of child reading

Figure 19.6 Storybook stained glass

Figure 19.7 Neon panel

window's size and outline it using a marker. Submit the butcher paper and the transparency to a local stained glass studio for a price quote. If the window is a memorial for a community or library leader, local artisans may volunteer their time, or you may designate the project for possible donations in a funeral notice. Friends of the Library groups may choose to fundraise to commemorate a historic library milestone or anniversary with a window. Install over or behind the existing safety glass already in the library.

Neon. For a more modern use of glass, consider neon. Neon is visible for hundreds of feet on the interior of a building. Neon is far more affordable than stained glass, at only one-tenth of the cost, but upkeep and repairs tend to be ongoing costs. A 12-square-foot window might cost $500 or less, but budget $100 per year for maintenance even though you probably will not spend that much. It is a good idea to generate both the initial cost and four years' worth of maintenance at the beginning of the project. Use a screwdriver to install or remove a lightweight neon landscape from an existing sidelight library window.

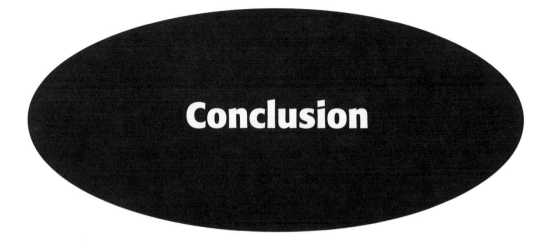

Conclusion

James Bond, of double-O fame, is a daring and inventive problem solver. A Shoestring Librarian can rightfully claim double-O stature as well: optimistic opportunist. It is a perspective well-suited to the economic climate. The glass is not half full; it is *brimming*. The 421 hints in this book have two things in common: they support a stimulating student habitat and vigorous habits of mind. A Shoestring Librarian models the practice of using retrieved, evaluated information and ideas to create an upbeat school environment for students and staff.

That combines well with retrieved, repurposed, and recycled materials including media, furniture, and art described in this book. Consistently challenge students until "how to," "make do," and "can do" reverberate in their skulls. Eventually while they are transforming the library into their work and study space, they will transform themselves into that rare creature: richly competent individuals.

James Bond, of double-O fame, is a daring and innovative problem solver. A Shoestring Librarian can rightfully claim double-O stature as well: optimistic opportunist. The glass is not half full; it is *brimming*.

INDEX

U

Union benefits, 27
Upshot ceiling paint, 98

W

Walkabout, 9
Webcasts, 29

Weeding, 10, 107
Window clings, 127, 128
Wind-up flashlight, 52
Worksheets, 39

Y

Yard stick or meter stick, 20
Y cable, 8